SMACC NASTY

Hip Hop Culture Entertainment

Community

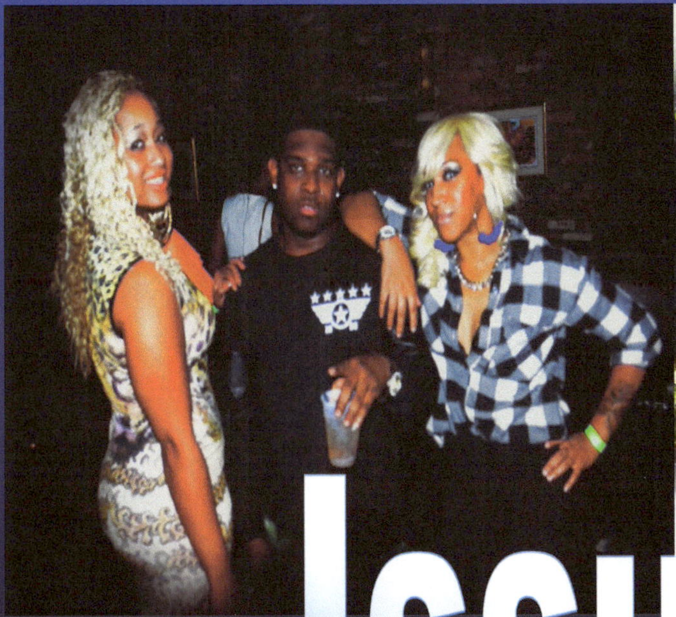

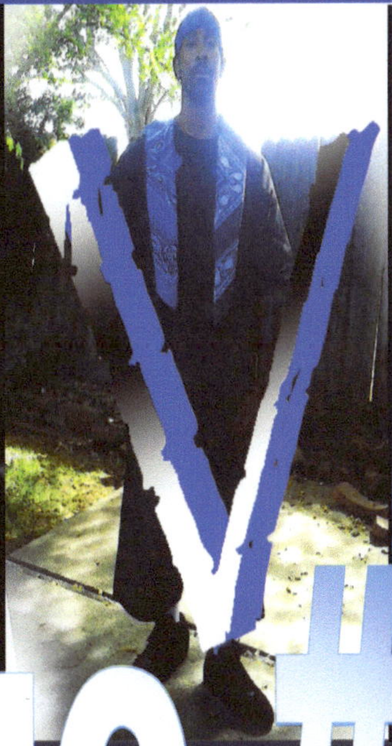

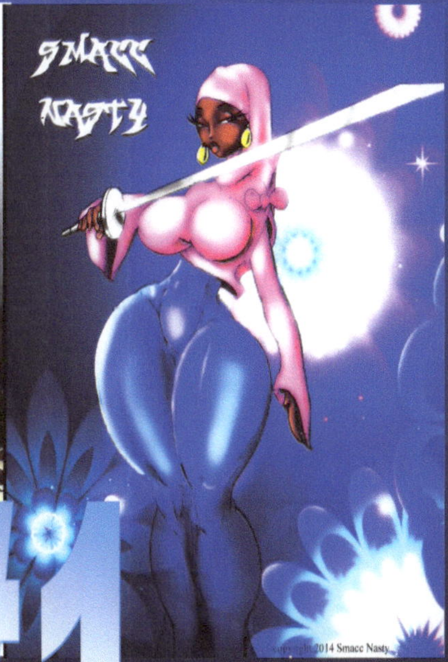

Issue #1

Table of Contents

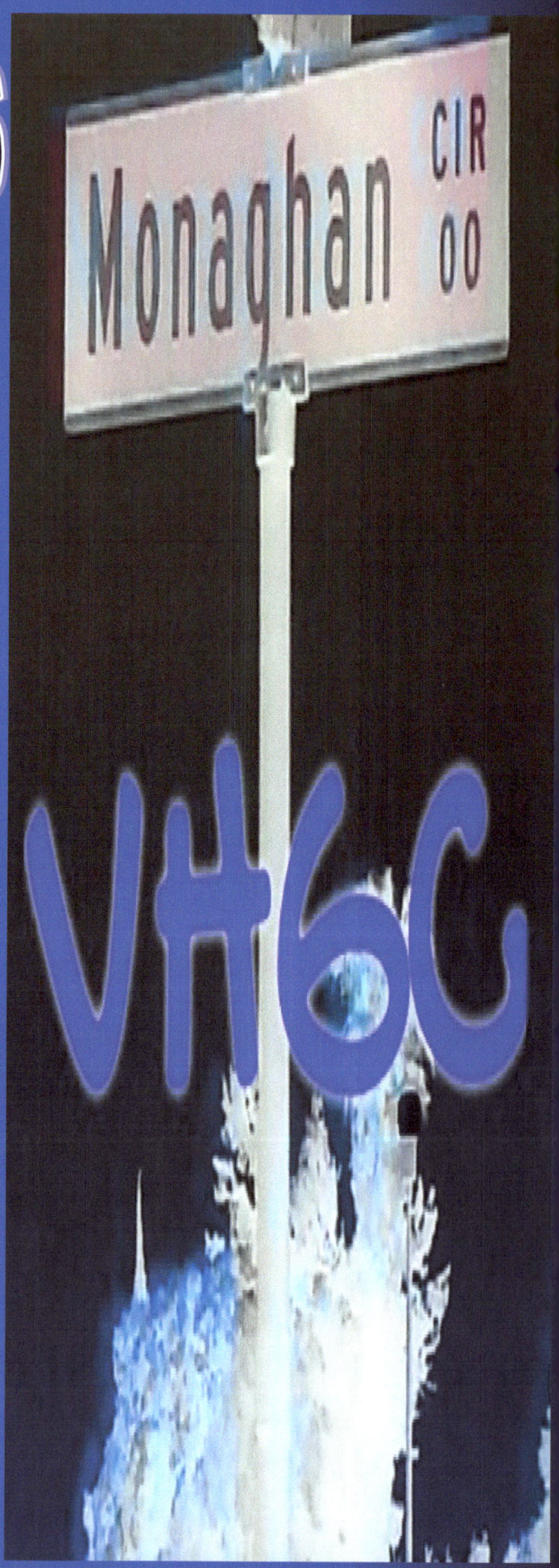

Smacc Nasty Straight

Copyright 2014 Smacc Nasty

Art Design: Yehezqel Ben Yisrael

Photography: Yehezqel Ben Yisrael

Editing: Yehezqel Ben Yisrael

Contact info: smaccnasty@yahoo.com

Office Phone: (916)999-0371

WWW.smaccnasty.com

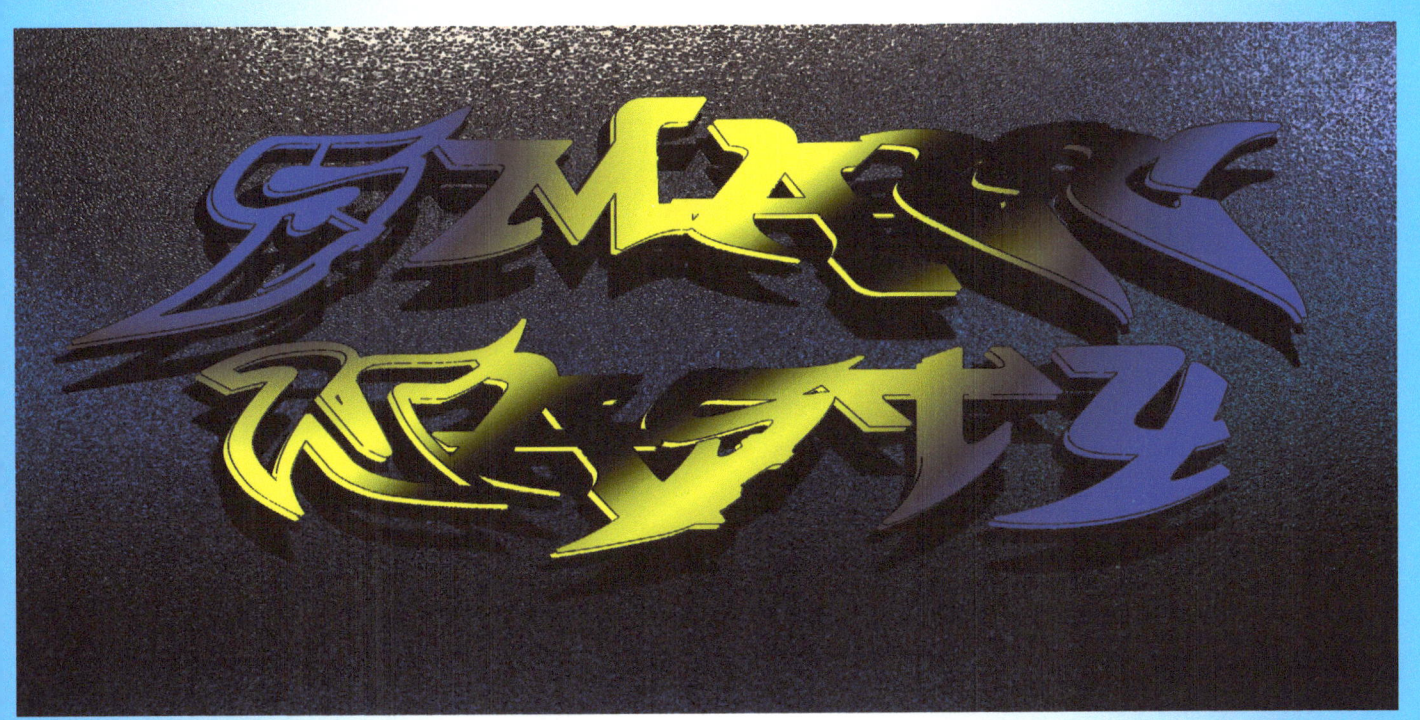

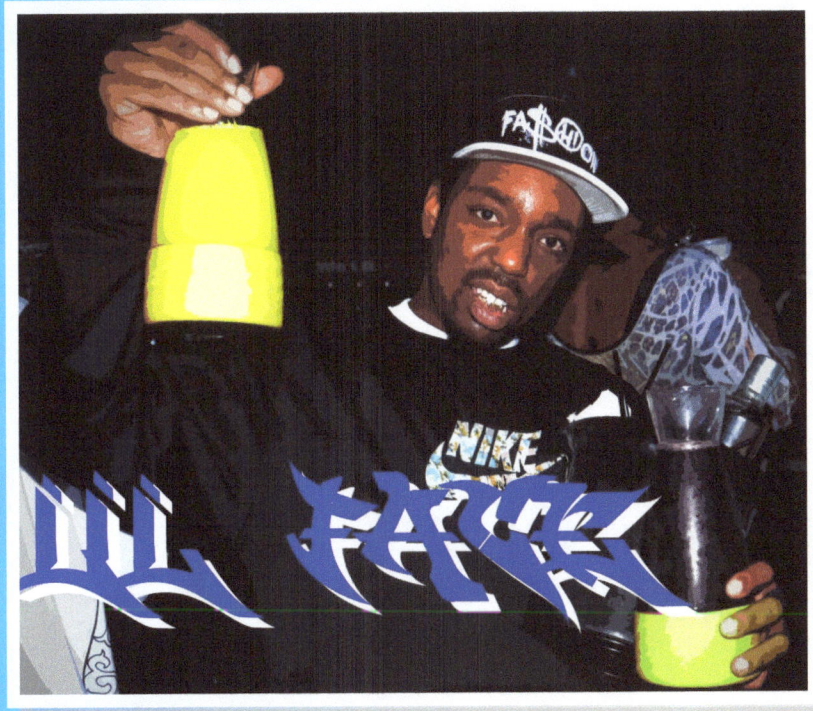

Lil Face from Valley Hi, South Sacramento, California is putting it down for the turf. The music he creates is "Gangsta". His new video, produced by Smacc Nasty can be viewed on our website www.smaccnasty.com.

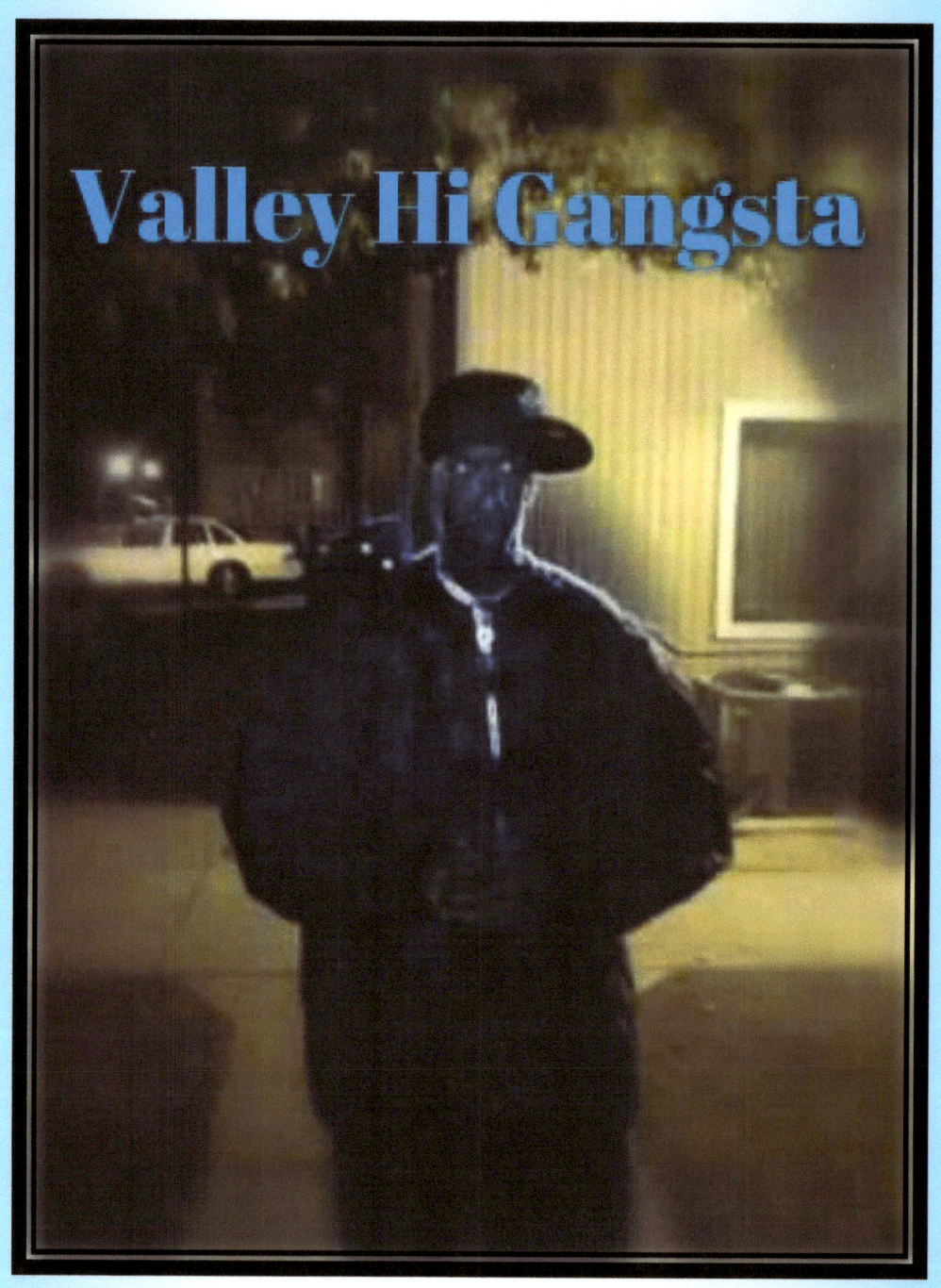

Valley Hi Gangsta

The Fighting Spirit of a True Warrior

VHGC

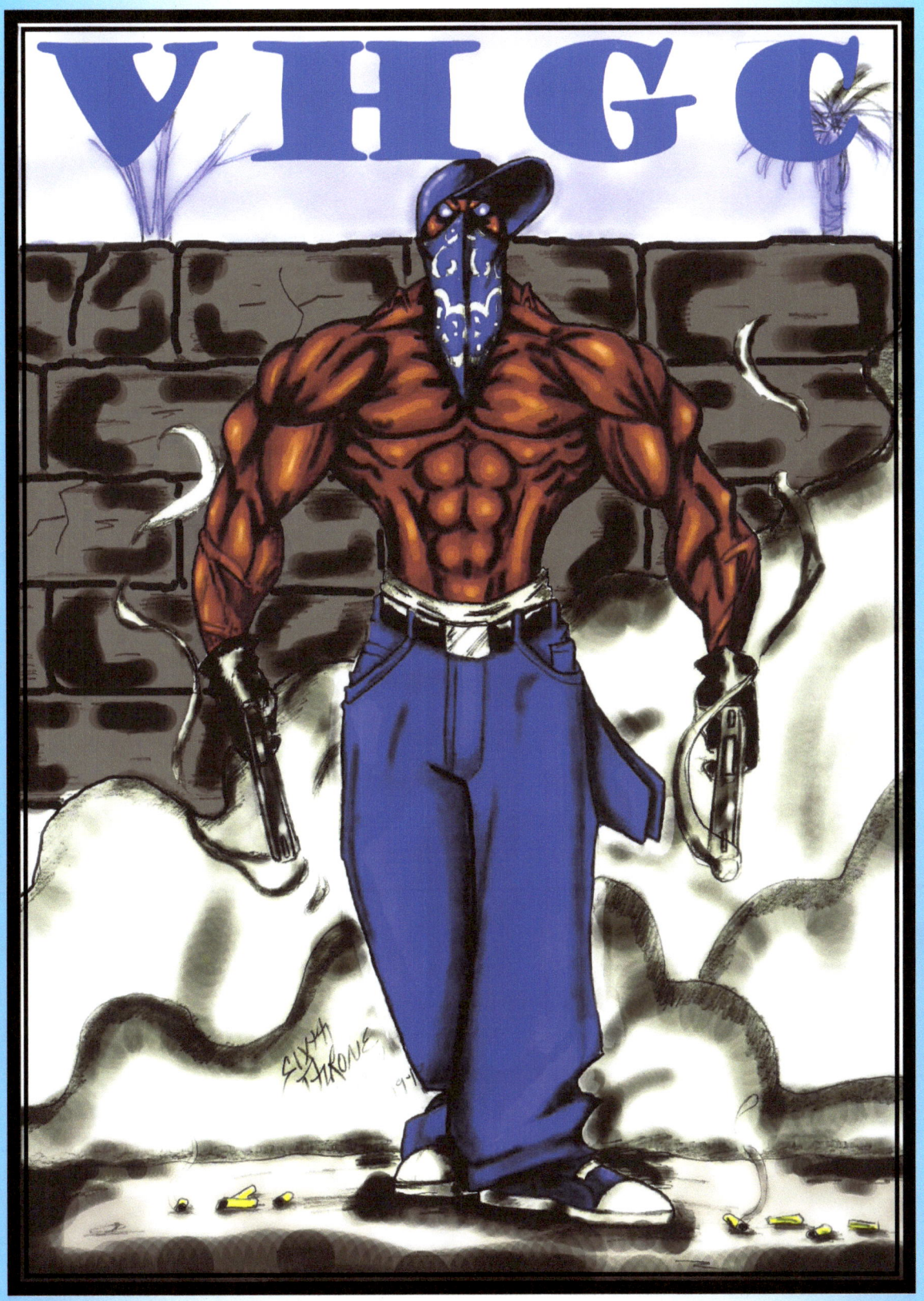

B.G. Hi Devil Loco

Meet some of the Locs from the capital city of the state of California.

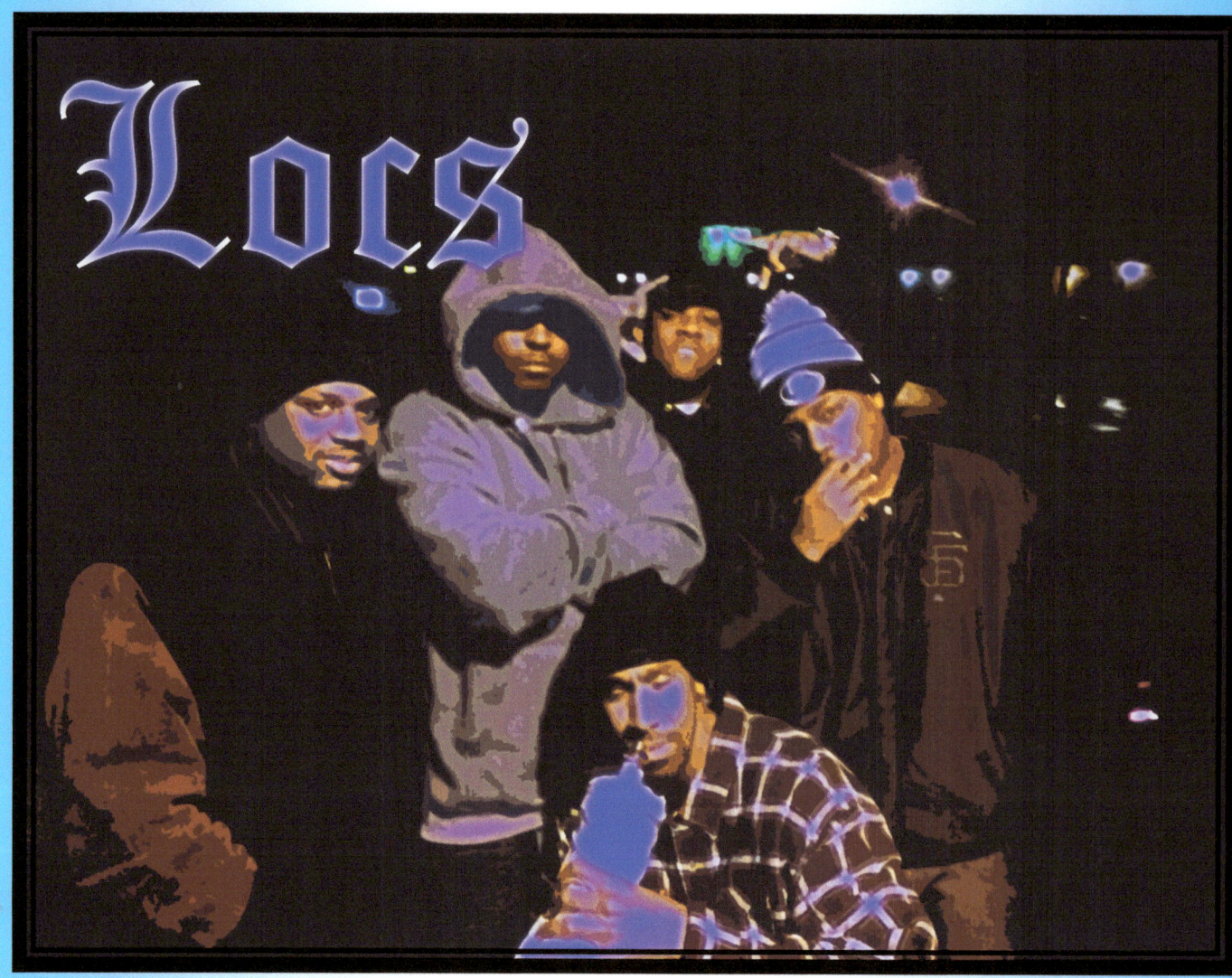

The Gangsta Element

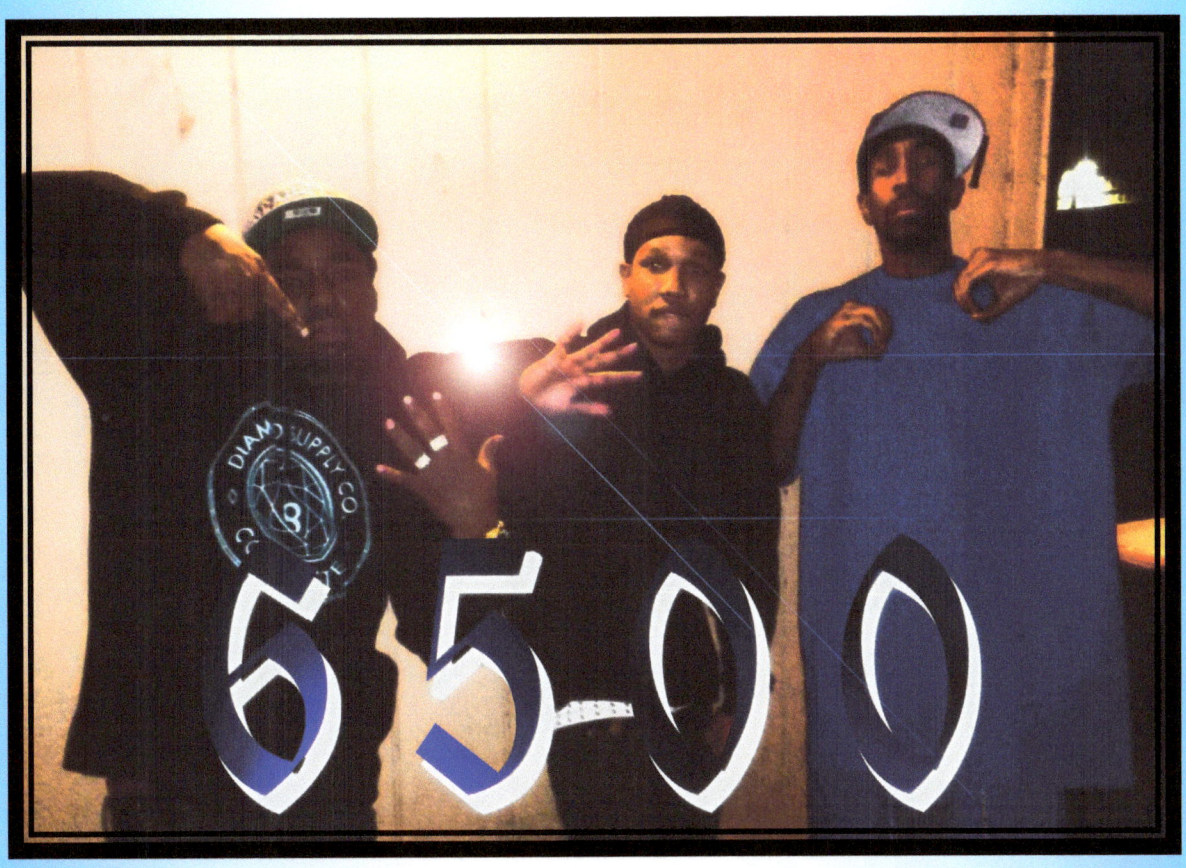

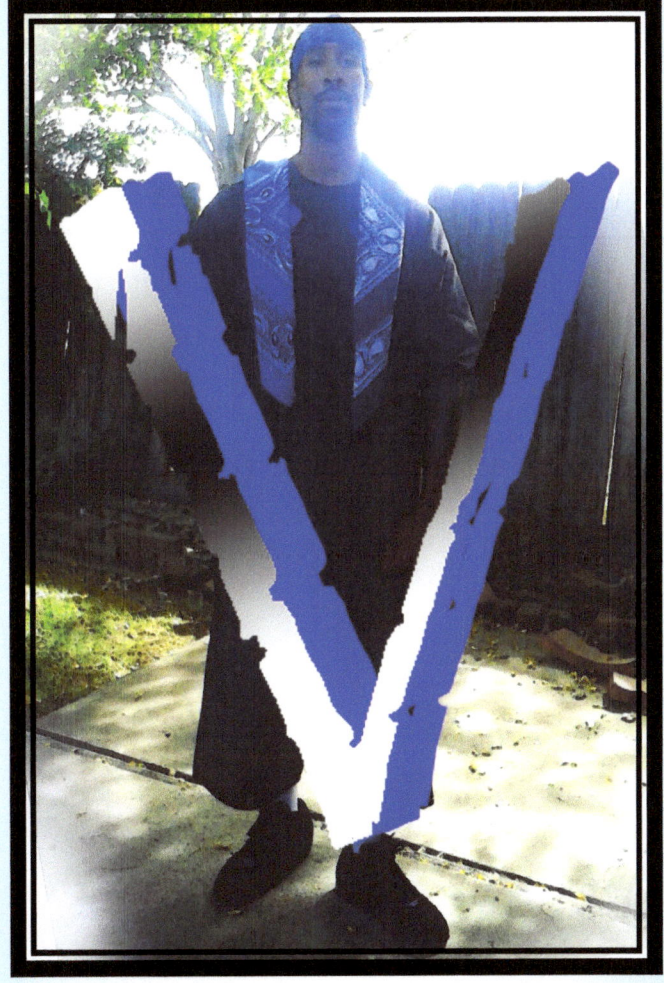

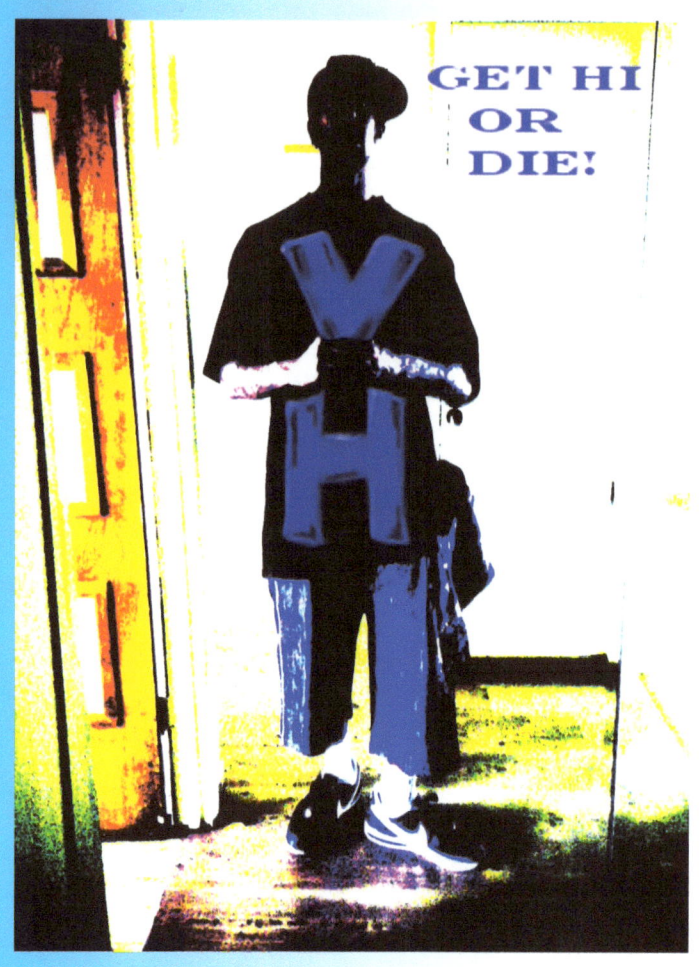

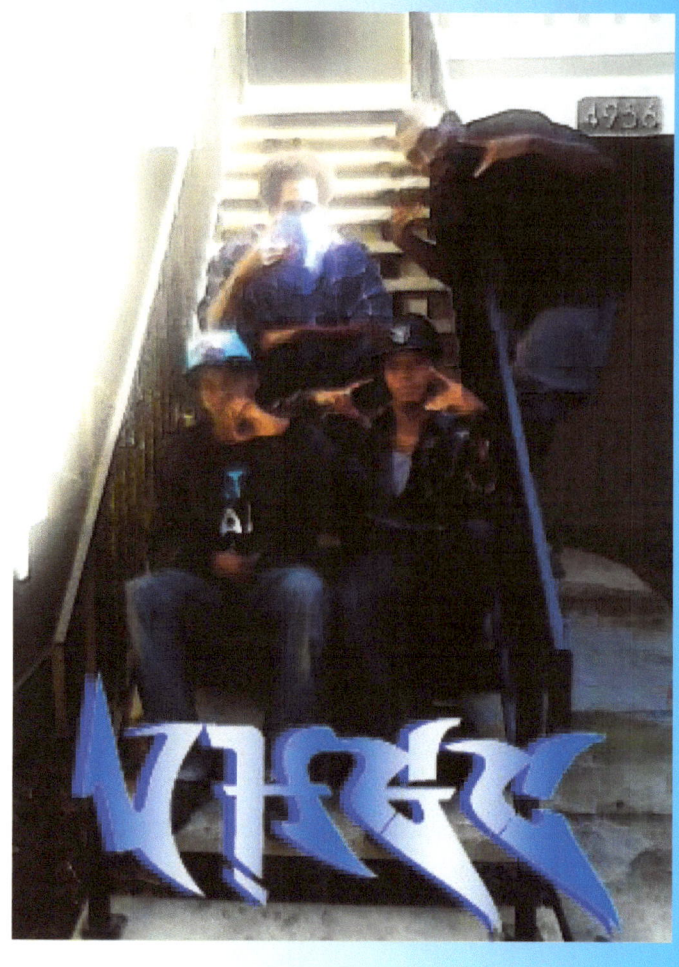

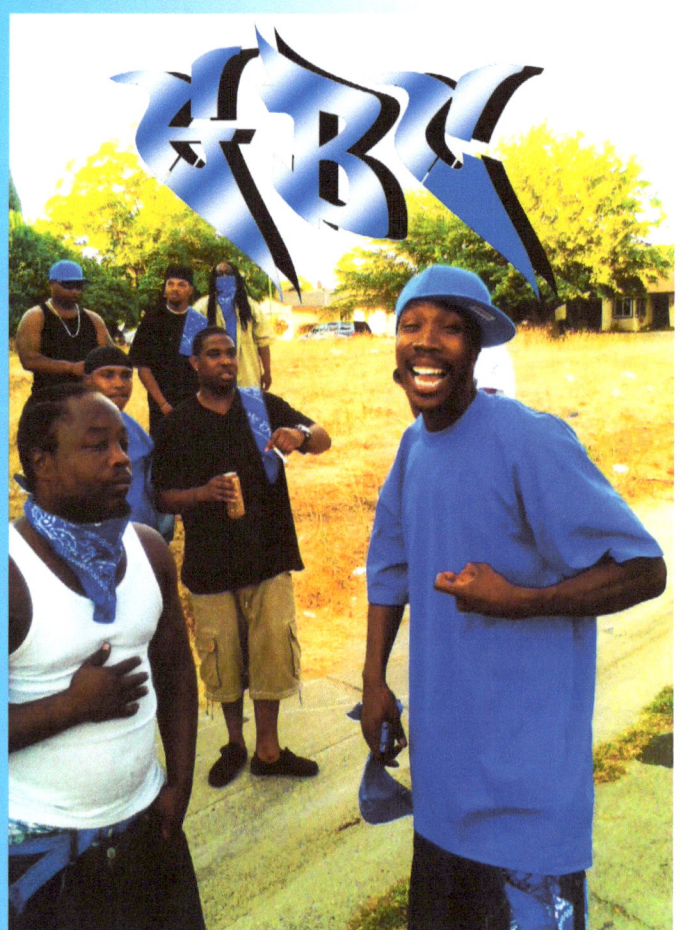

These young black men strive to achieve greatness in their communities by encouraging unity, education, integrity, and discipline within the family.

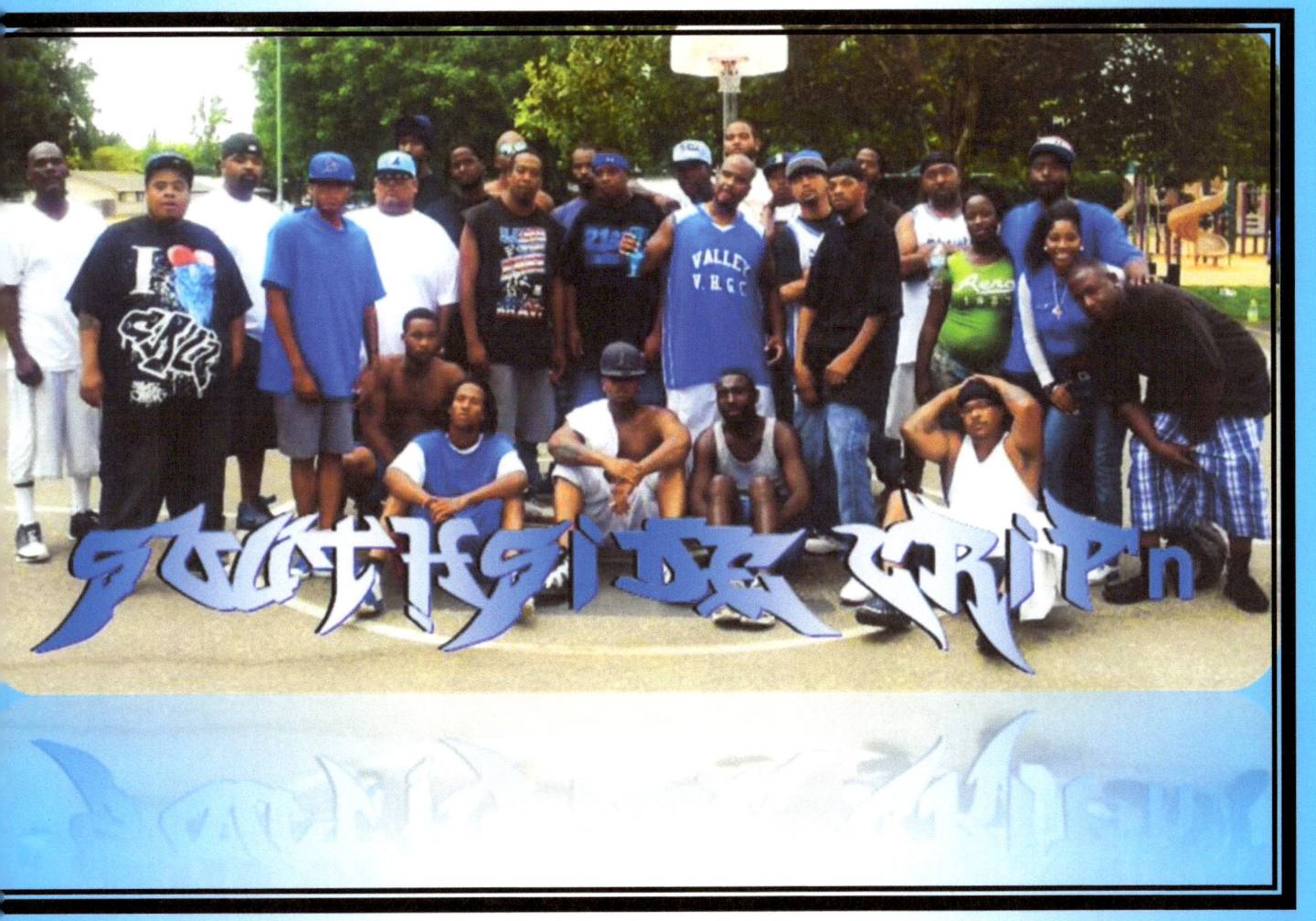

Unity of the militant brothas in the community is what Crip'n is all about.

Black American

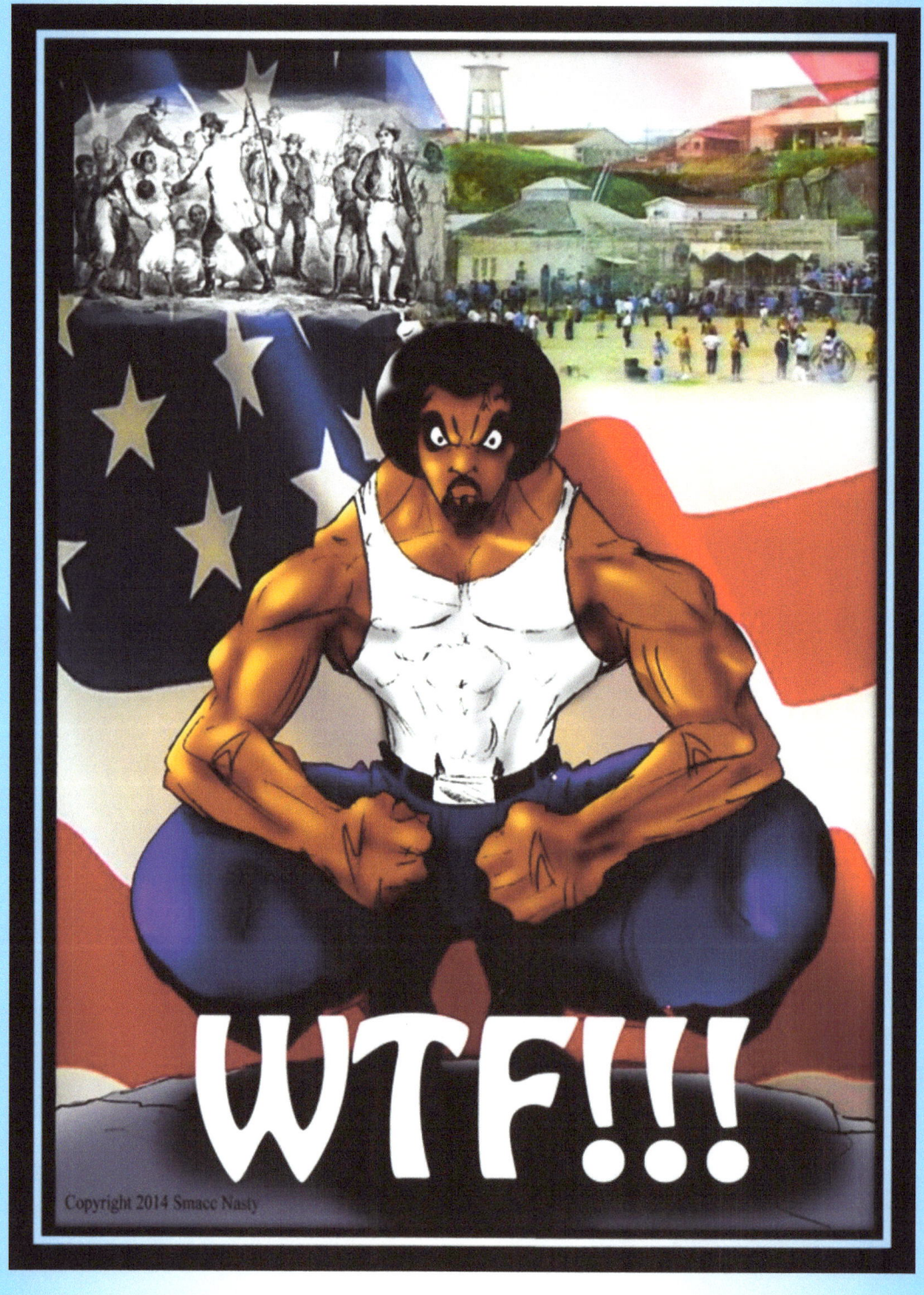

What does it mean to be black in America? Through the eyes of this young African-American male it means to be detestable, violent, unintelligent, and hopeless in the eyes of the rest of the foreigners who migrated to this land. Most of the nations that migrated to north America did so with the hopes and dreams of living a better life, with freedom from the oppression from their countries or for the opportunity to increase their standard of living. Freedom to live one's life to the fullest is what this country is supposed to be all about, except for the black Africans of West Africa. The black Africans were not meant to have freedom. They were merely hauled to the Americas in slave ships to be nothing more than animal-like slaves and servants. After much blood, sweat, tears and murder of nearly 100 million Africans, today the Africans in America are free—or are they? Today the jails and prison systems house nearly 20 percent of the African-American male population, forcing them to do slave labor for no pay or very miniscule pay, while many more are tortured and killed in the streets of America by law-enforcement agencies and Ku Klux Klan members. Intellectual Klan members in alliance with other "haters" from European and Arab countries continue to oppress and enslave black Africans physically and mentally. Some African-Americans feel that they are free just because they are not getting whipped and burned alive, and because they find themselves feeding from the scraps under "master's" table (a little job working in one of their businesses). This is not freedom this is Stockholm syndrome. Wikipedia states, "**Stockholm syndrome**, or **capture-bonding**, is a psychological phenomenon in which hostages express empathy and sympathy and have positive feelings toward their captors, sometimes to the point of defending and identifying with them. These feelings are generally considered irrational in light of the danger or risk endured by the victims, who essentially mistake a lack of abuse from their captors for an act of kindness."

BLACK MAN AND WOMAN YOU ARE NOT FREE!!! THE FIGHT MUST CONTINUE!!!

Ladies and Gentleman...
The Man of the Hour

Tiny Cheese

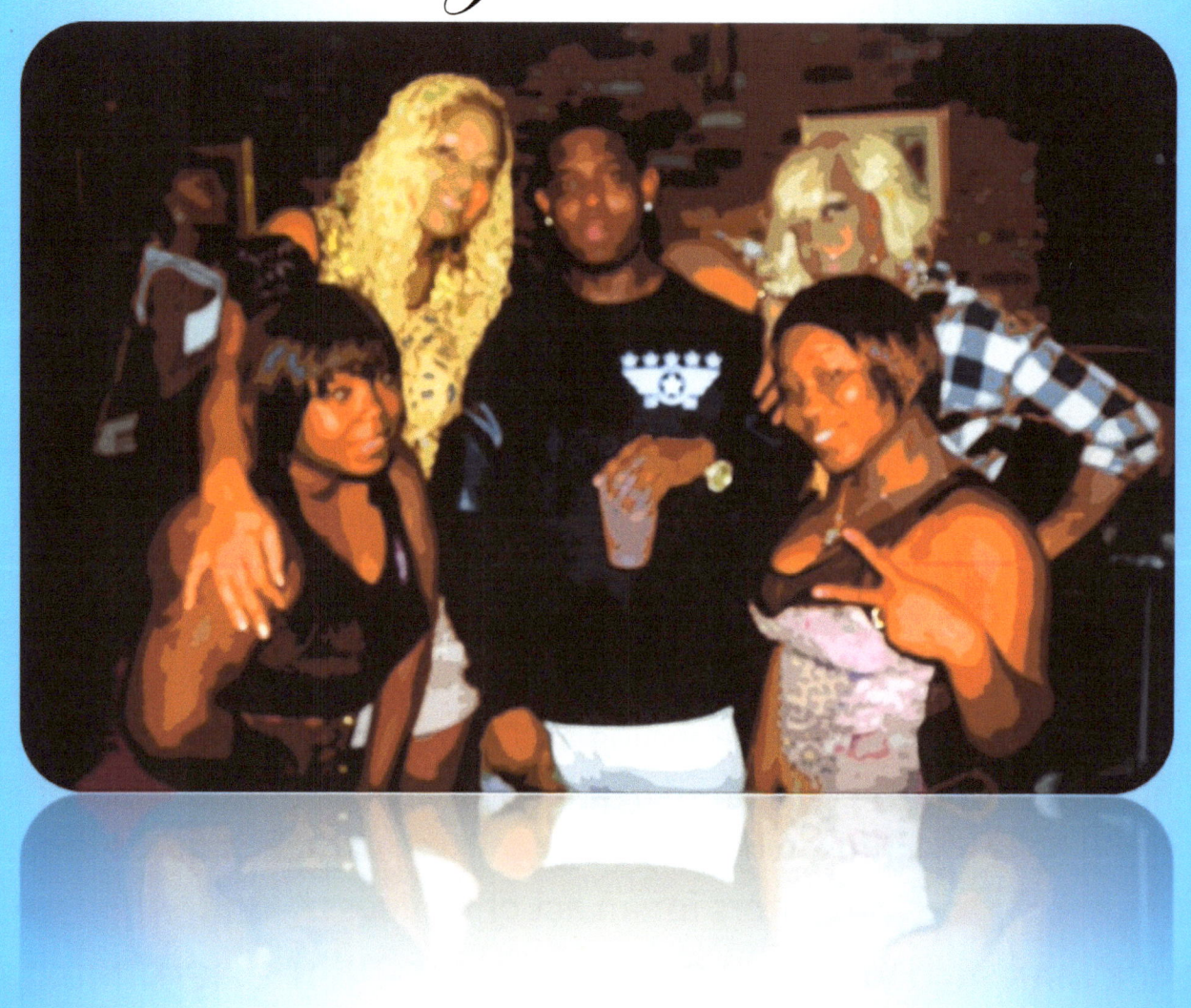

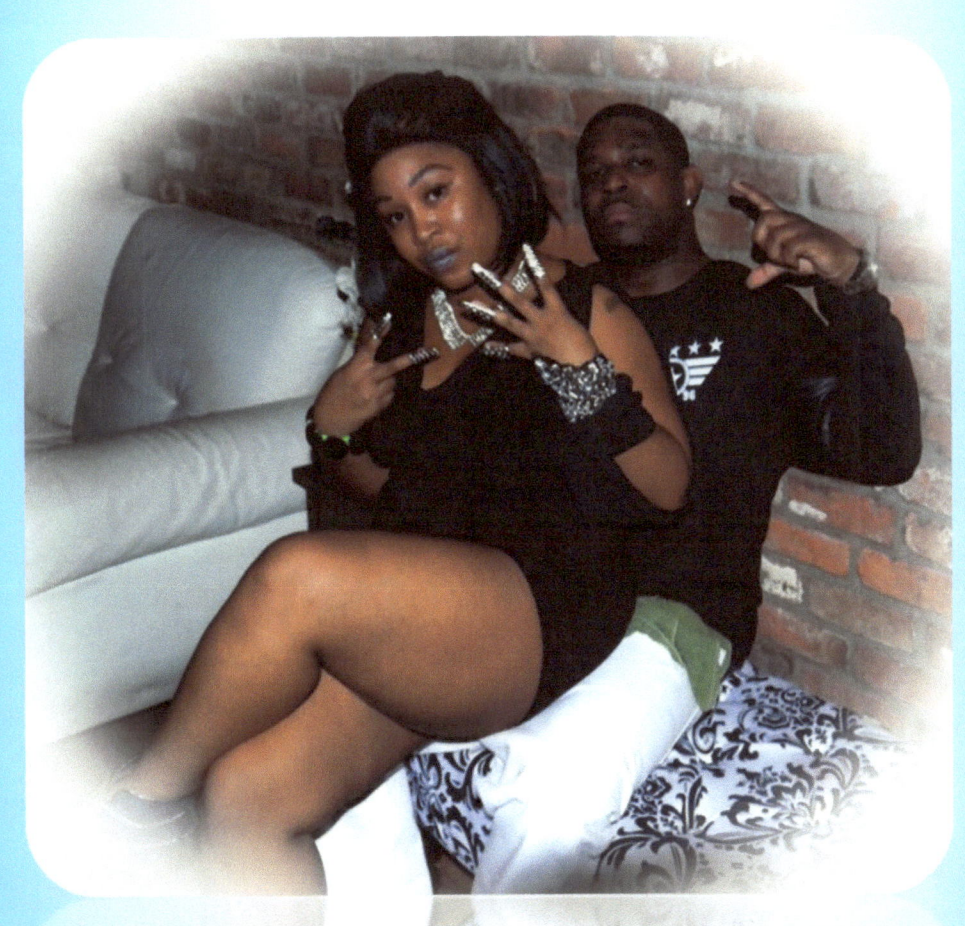

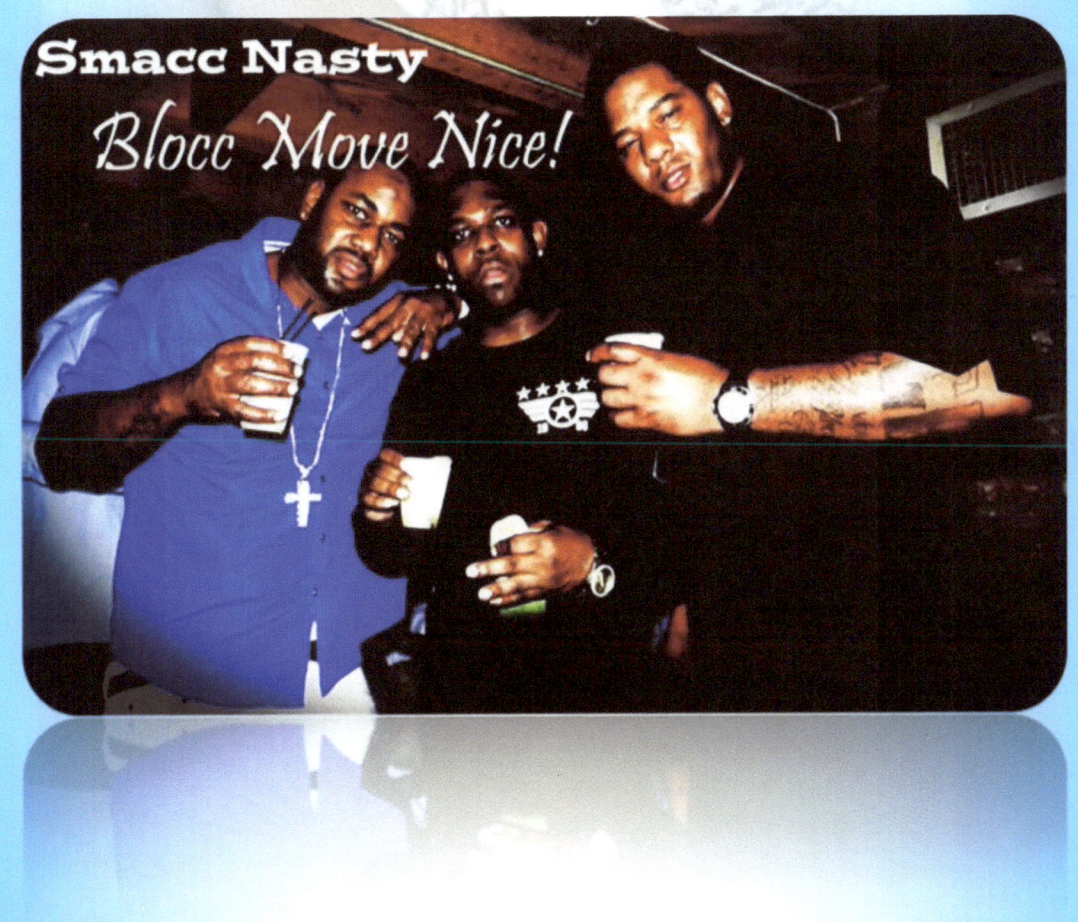

13

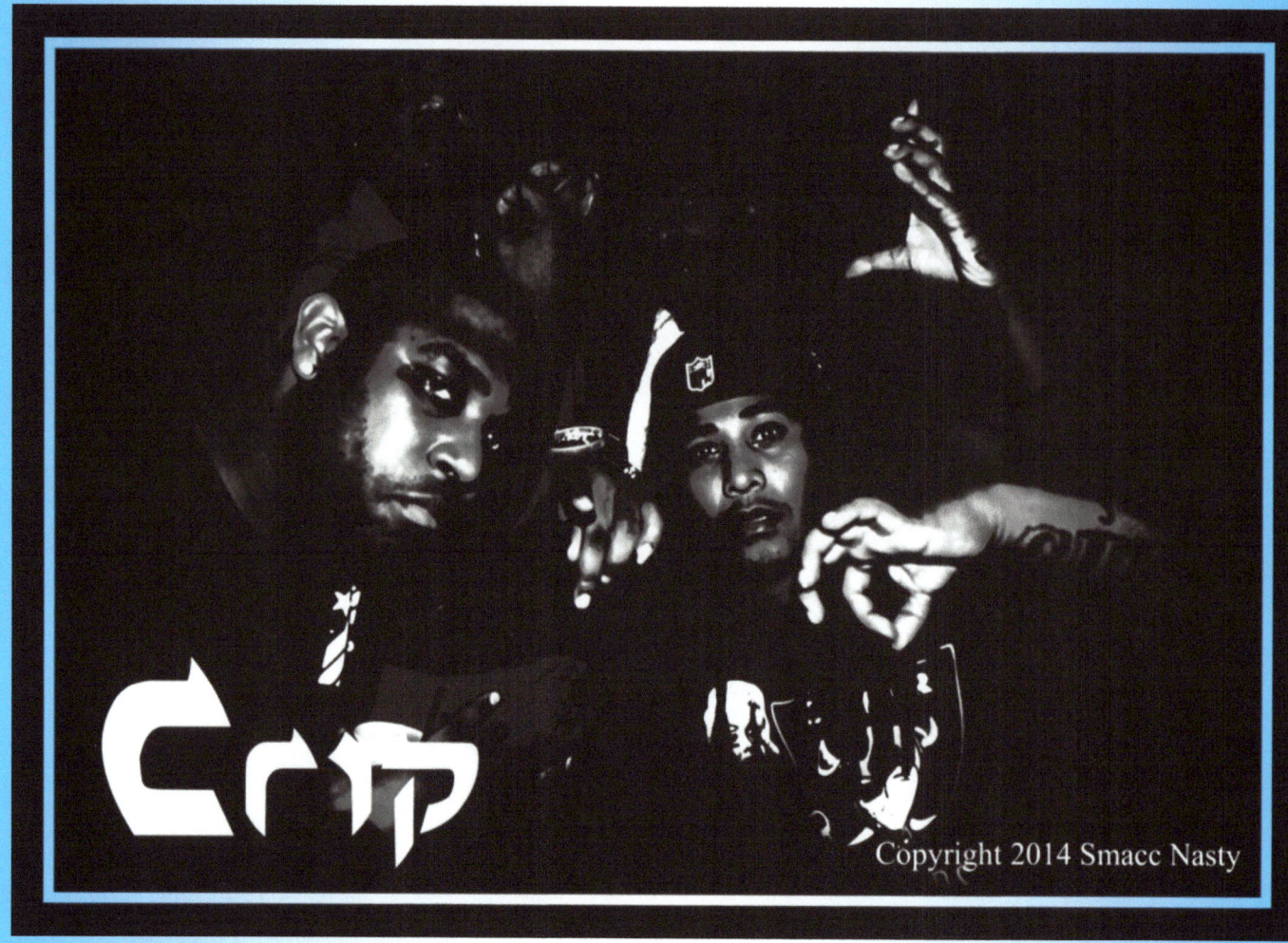

This is one brotha that knows how to move nice.

The Bloodfist

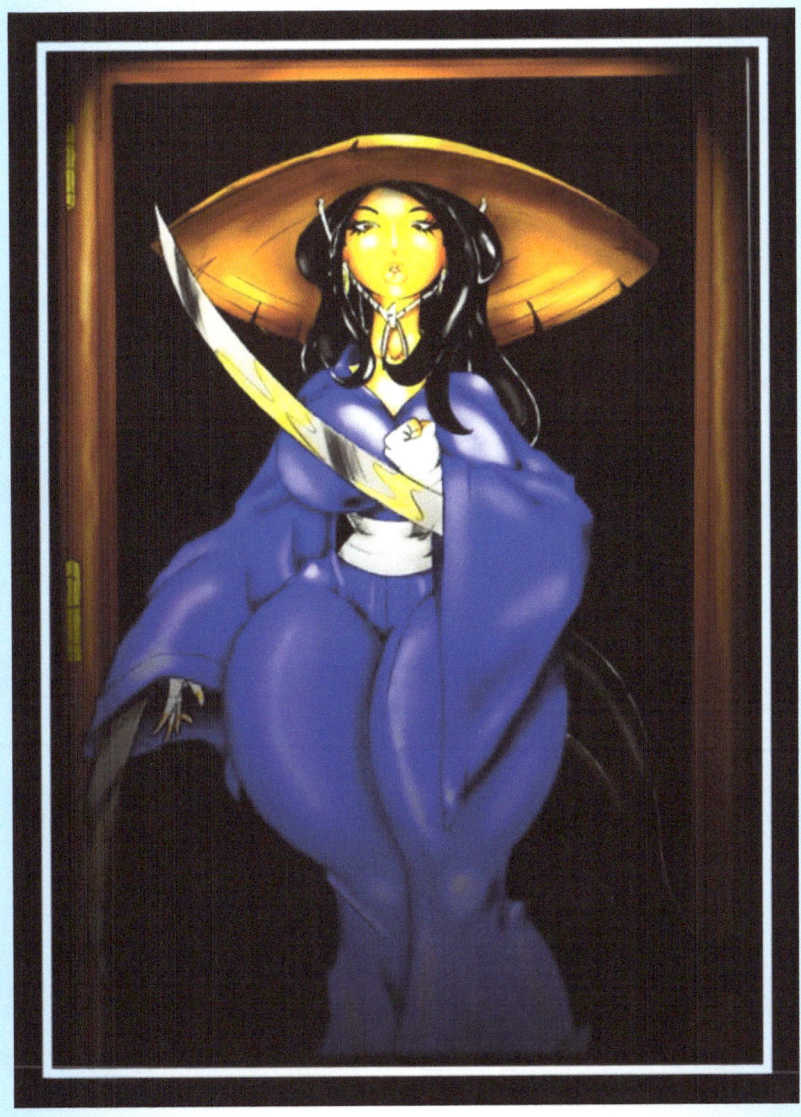

Bloodfist is a spy that specializes in search and rescue and all out sabatage and destruction. Her goal is to defend the lives of the innocent and to destroy terrorist organizations and evil plots by governments.

Name: Shayoki Shaniqua Yamata Genshin aka Bi Ch'uan Fa (Blue Fist Law) aka The Bloodfist

Born: 1895

Birthplace: China

Height: 5'7"

Weight: 185 lbs.

Bio: Bloodfist (Shaniqua) was born and raised in a small house knowing nothing about the world except for what her father and big sister told her. They lived in a small shack about a mile away from a river. From the age of 3 when she could somewhat comprehend what it meant to fight she 'played karate' with her dad and sister. Then at the age of 5 she studied seriously, then at the age of 10 she bloodied her big sisters nose sparring. At the age of 12 she bloodied her father's nose. Her father, whose name was Genshin Yamata, was a master of Ninjitsu. That same year her father sent her to study with an old Kung-Fu master by the name of Chi Shang who taught her Wing-Chun and Tai-Chi. She was extraordinarily gifted because she

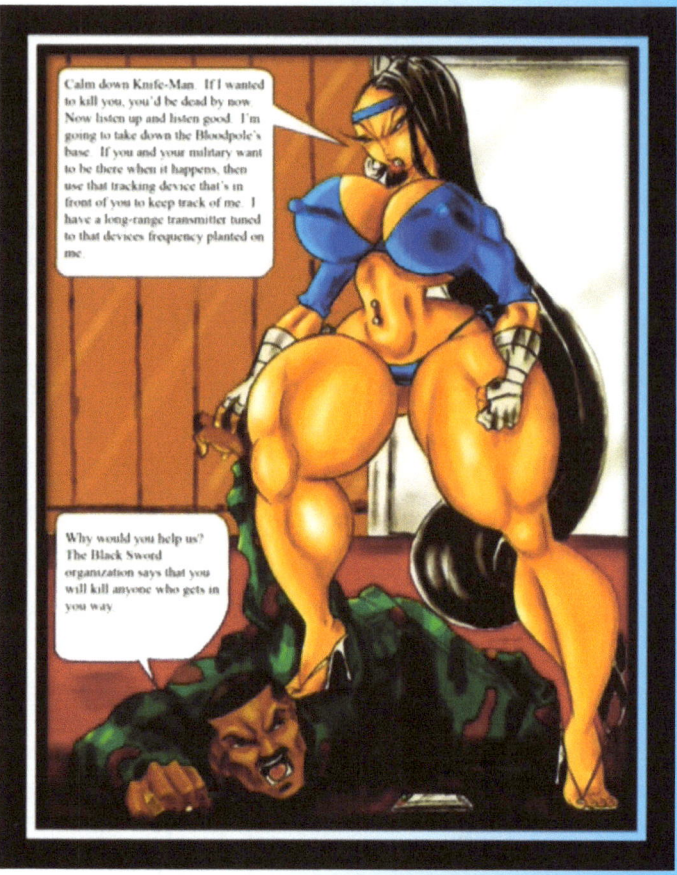

mastered both styles by time she was 16 and had fought every master in china and defeated them. When she returned to her father's home on her 17th birthday, her father was bursting with joy and pride. A month after being home her father was challenged to a duel by a mysterious ninja clan from Japan trying to make a name for themselves. The clan threatened to kill his two daughters if he declined. Not wanting to worry his daughters, he told them he was going to participate in an exhibition tournament to display his style and to make them proud. His daughters wanted to go, but it was forbidden. So he left for the tournament and never returned. A letter was delivered to them along with their father's sword. He was dead. Bloodfist's big sister blamed her for their father's death. Bloodfist cried herself to sleep that night. While she slept, kidnappers who were in cahoots with the clan that killed her father slipped into her bedroom and snatched her from her bed. Her big sister knew nothing of it because she was away visiting their father's grave. Bloodfist was taken to a terrorist group who was trying to overthrow the Japanese government. There she was operated and experimented on for over 7 years. The terrorist group targeted Bloodfist because of her fame for defeating all the great Kung-Fu masters of China. Her father was killed, so he wouldn't pursue them. They genetically enhanced the strength of her legs to the strength of 4 horses. They also gave her the ability to heal from any wound within minutes. The healing factor stopped her aging process. And finally they put liquid metal into her forearms enabling her to form razor sharp blades at will from her arms. Bloodfist was able to escape from the lab when it came under attack by the Japanese government. She killed the scientist, whose name was Professor Chan, that operated on her before she left. By the time she returned home everything was gone, including the house; therefore, she went to stay with her old master Chi Shang. She trained with him and she also searched for her sister. After 10 years Chi Shang died of old age. But before he died he invited an even older master to come and take on Bloodfist as his servant and student. The older master was centuries old in age but had the appearance of a young boy. The boy was the very first master of the deadly and powerful art called Nuba-Bujutsu. He was also a master of 20 other styles of fighting. Bloodfist became the servant and student of the young-old master whose name is Master Tien Lei also known as YeshaYahu, a Yehudi from the nation of Yisra'el. Bloodfist serves her master with an undying love and unwavering loyalty. After 40 years of training with her master she too became a master of the Nuba-Bujutsu art. And together they trained a small select group to battle the evils of

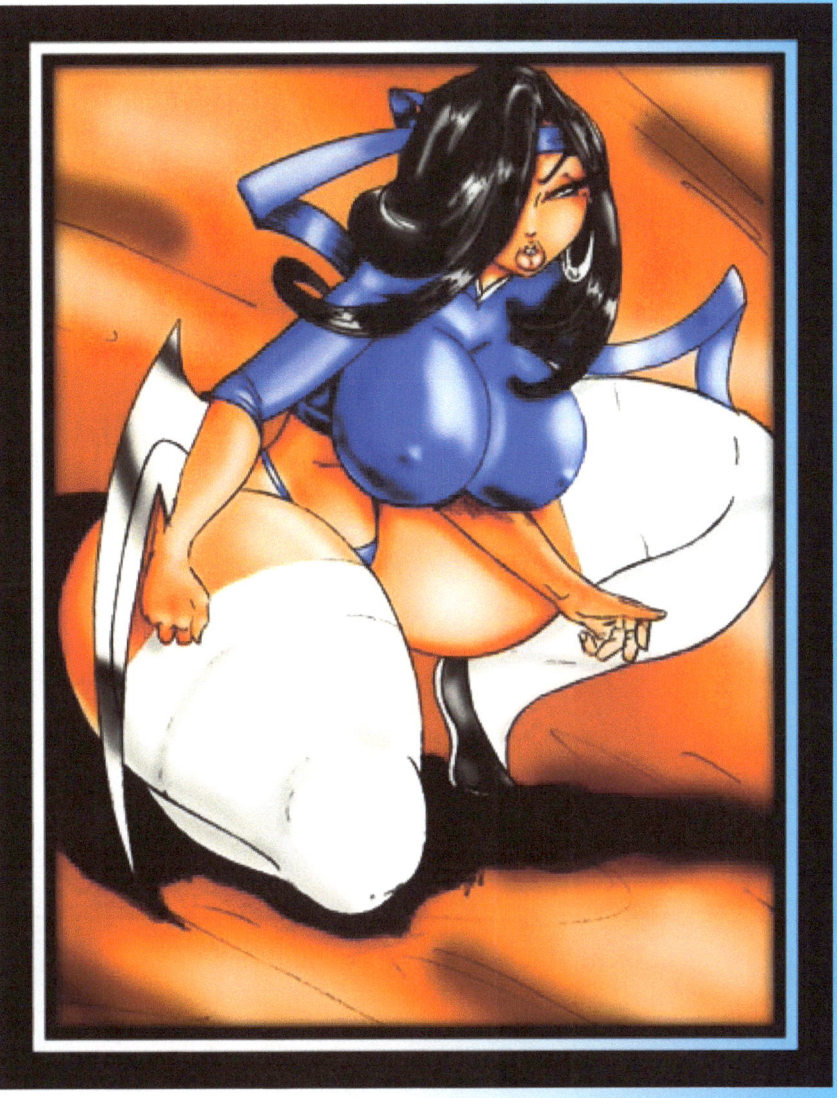

the world, evils that normal men cannot fight against or are just too afraid to fight against. They fight legendary and mythical battles. The battles are so unbelievable that the average person doesn't believe that the battles ever really took place or that Bloodfist and her master even really exist. The belief in the legend of Bloodfist is very small and the belief in her master, the master of the Nuba-Bujutsu arts is even smaller. But there are a few that Know. Those few that know either seek to be trained by The Bloodfist and her master and join them in their fight, or they seek to kill and destroy them, because it is they who prevent ambitious men, demons and demon possessed men from destroying the world.

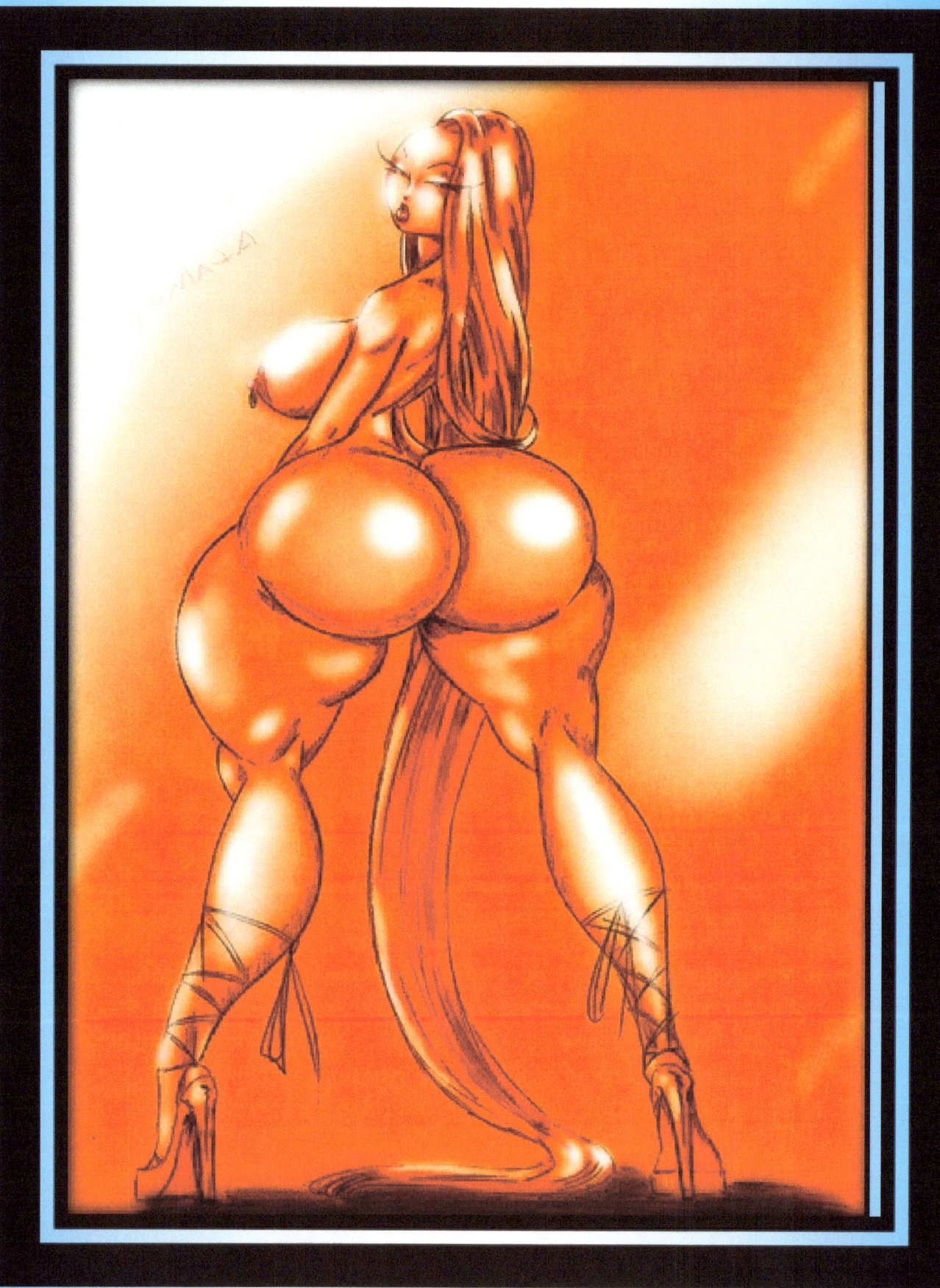

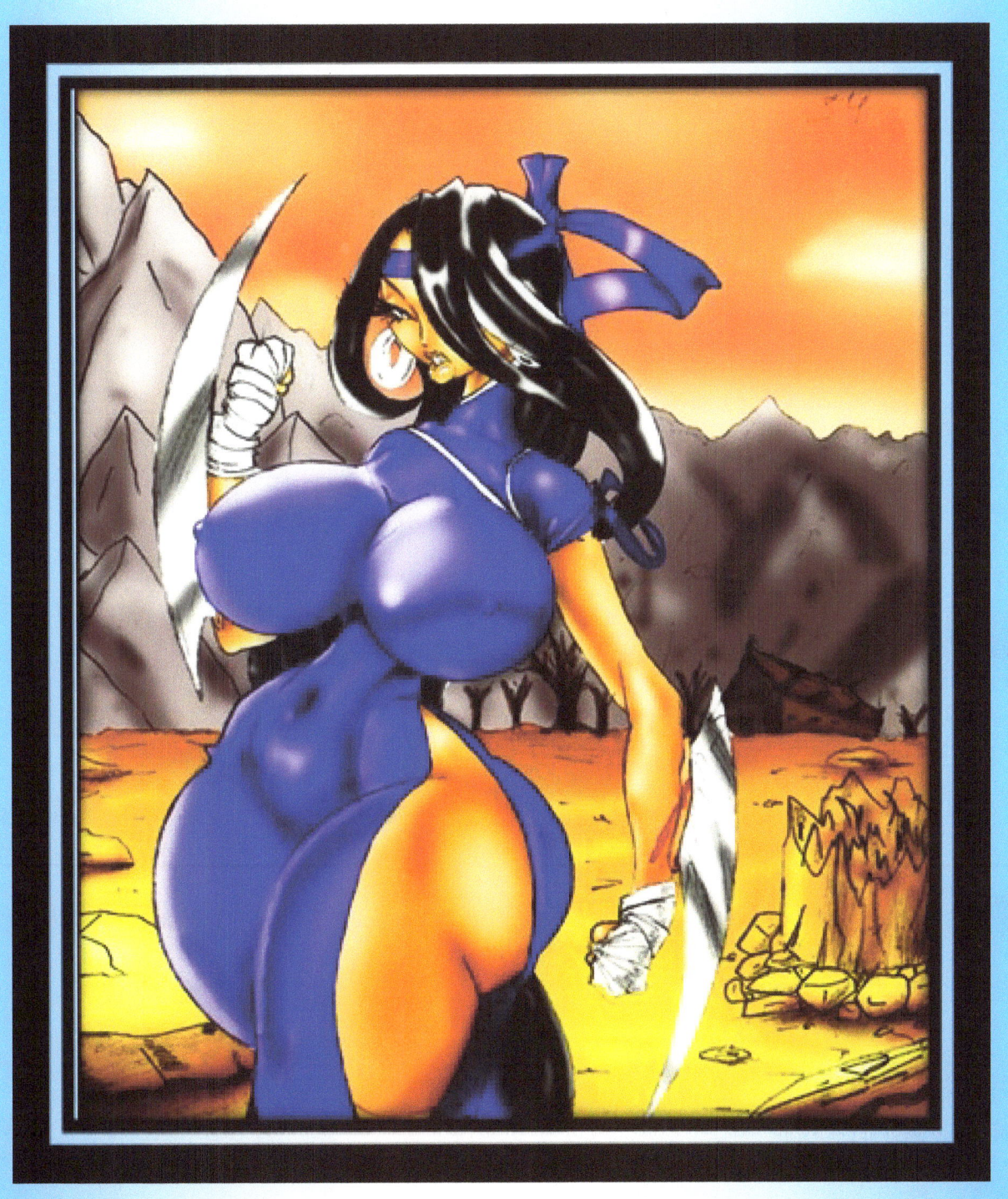

Bi Chu'an Fa
The Blood Fist

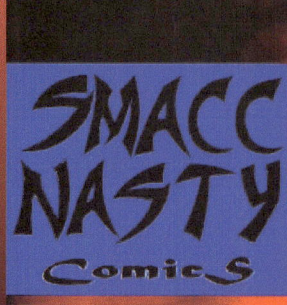

Ruakh of the Fist

Death Angel Tamica 1

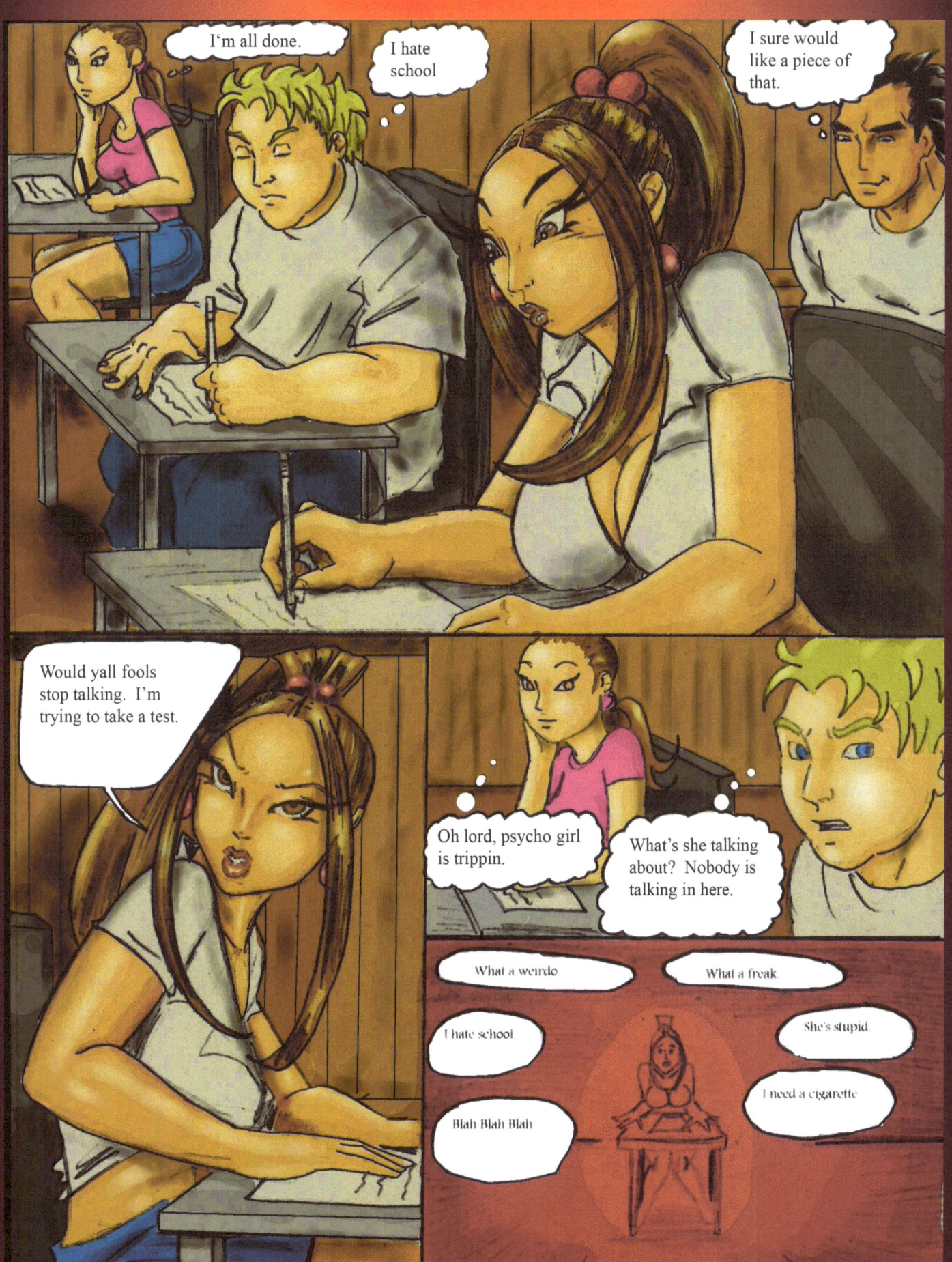

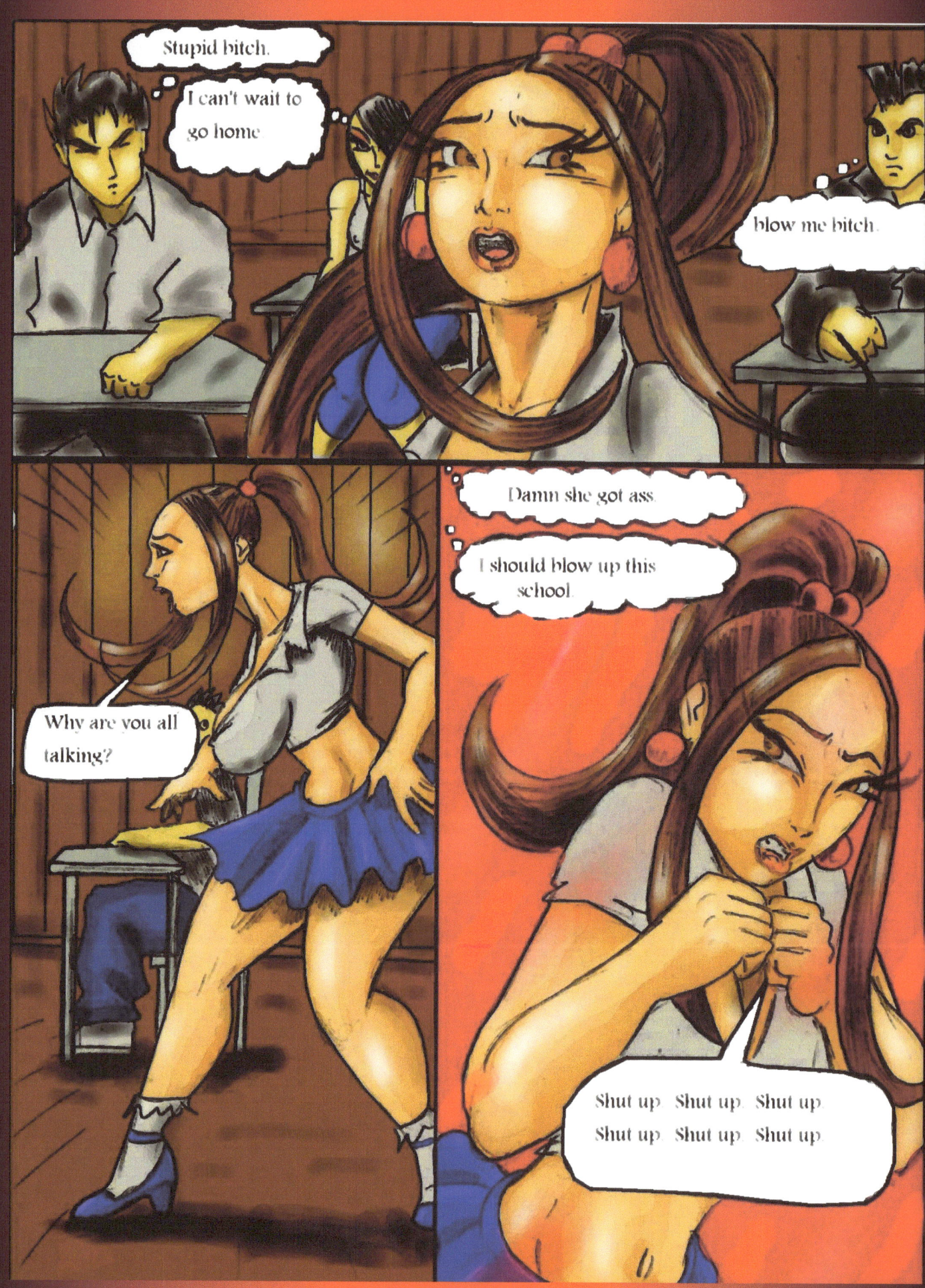

22

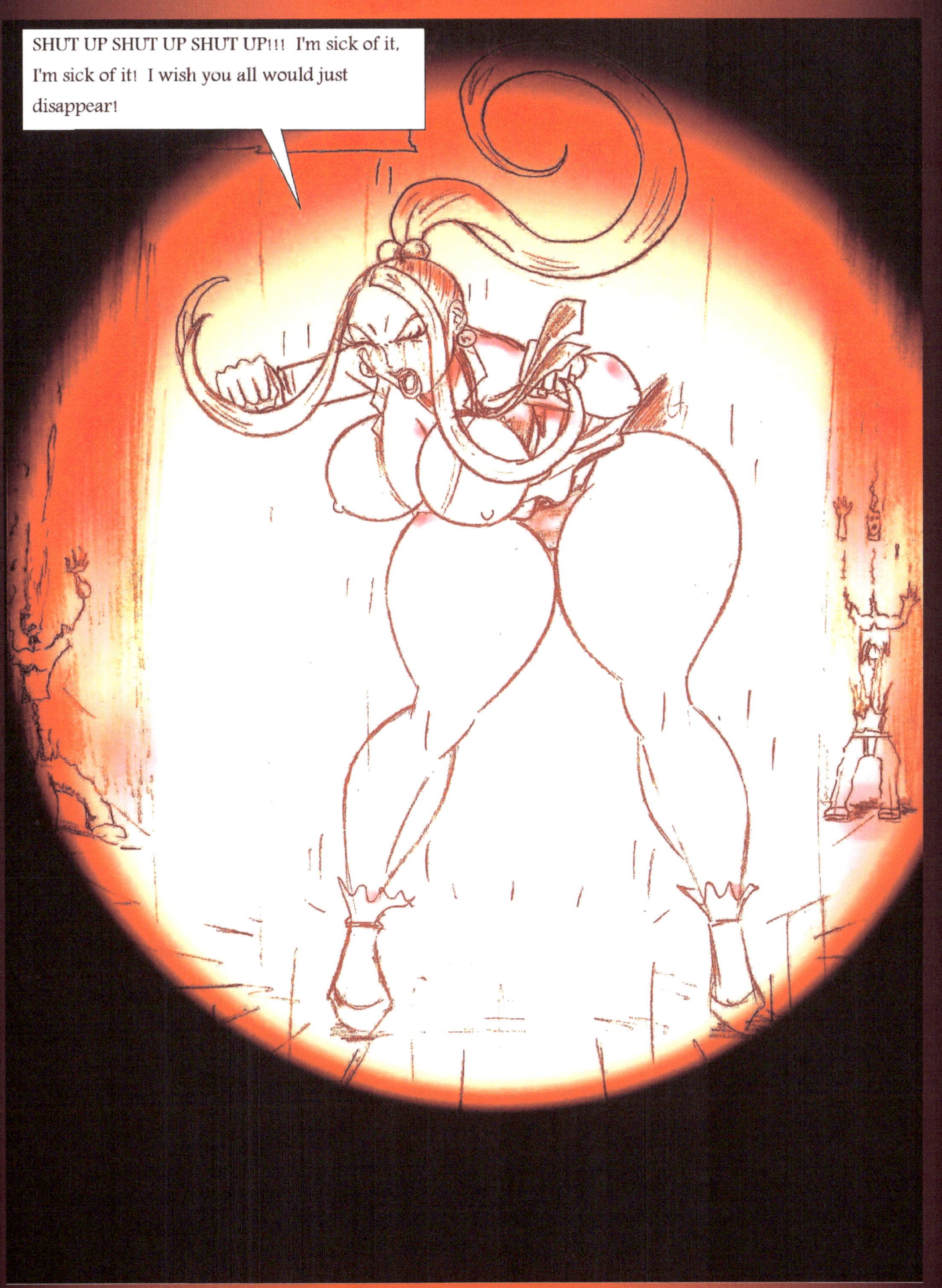

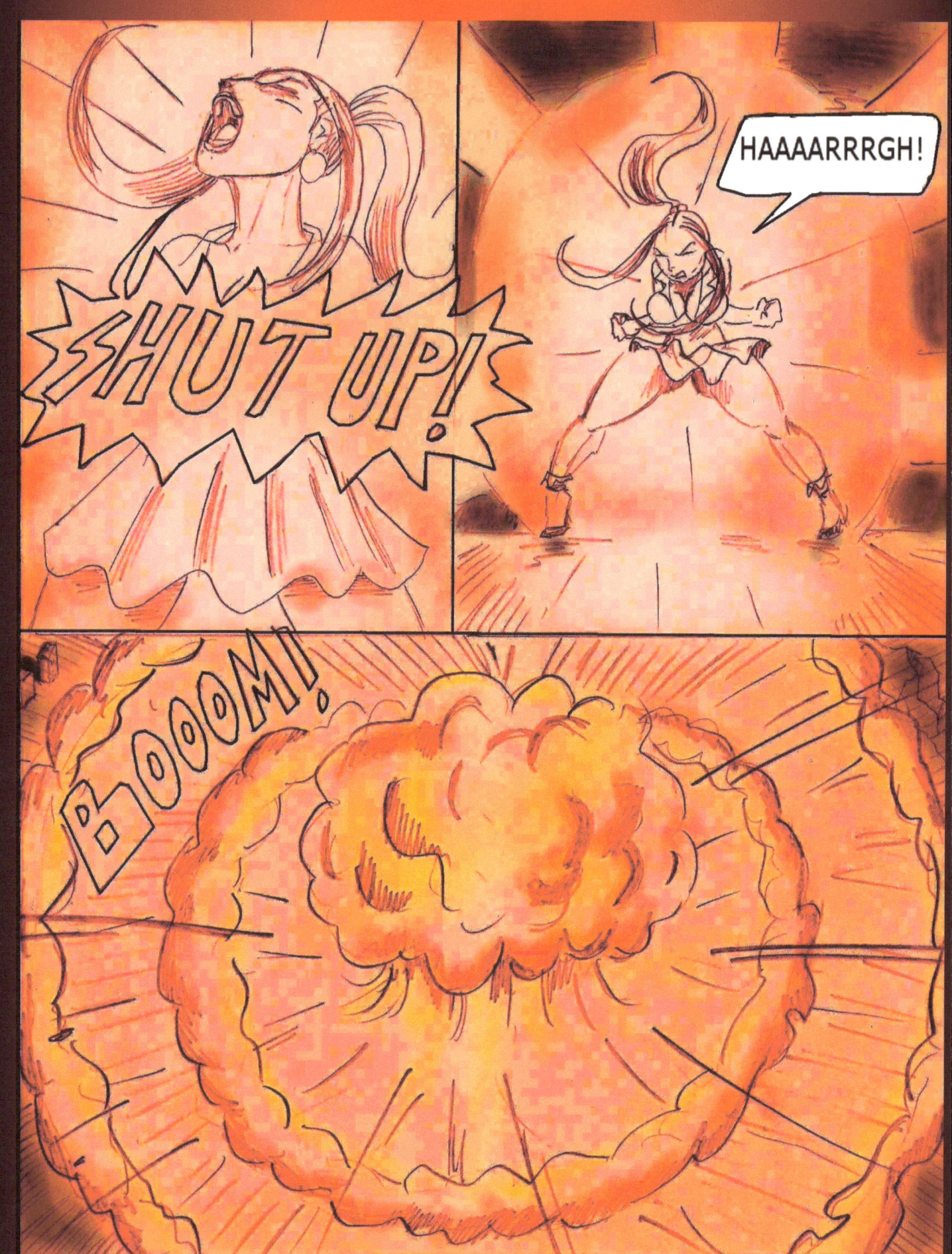

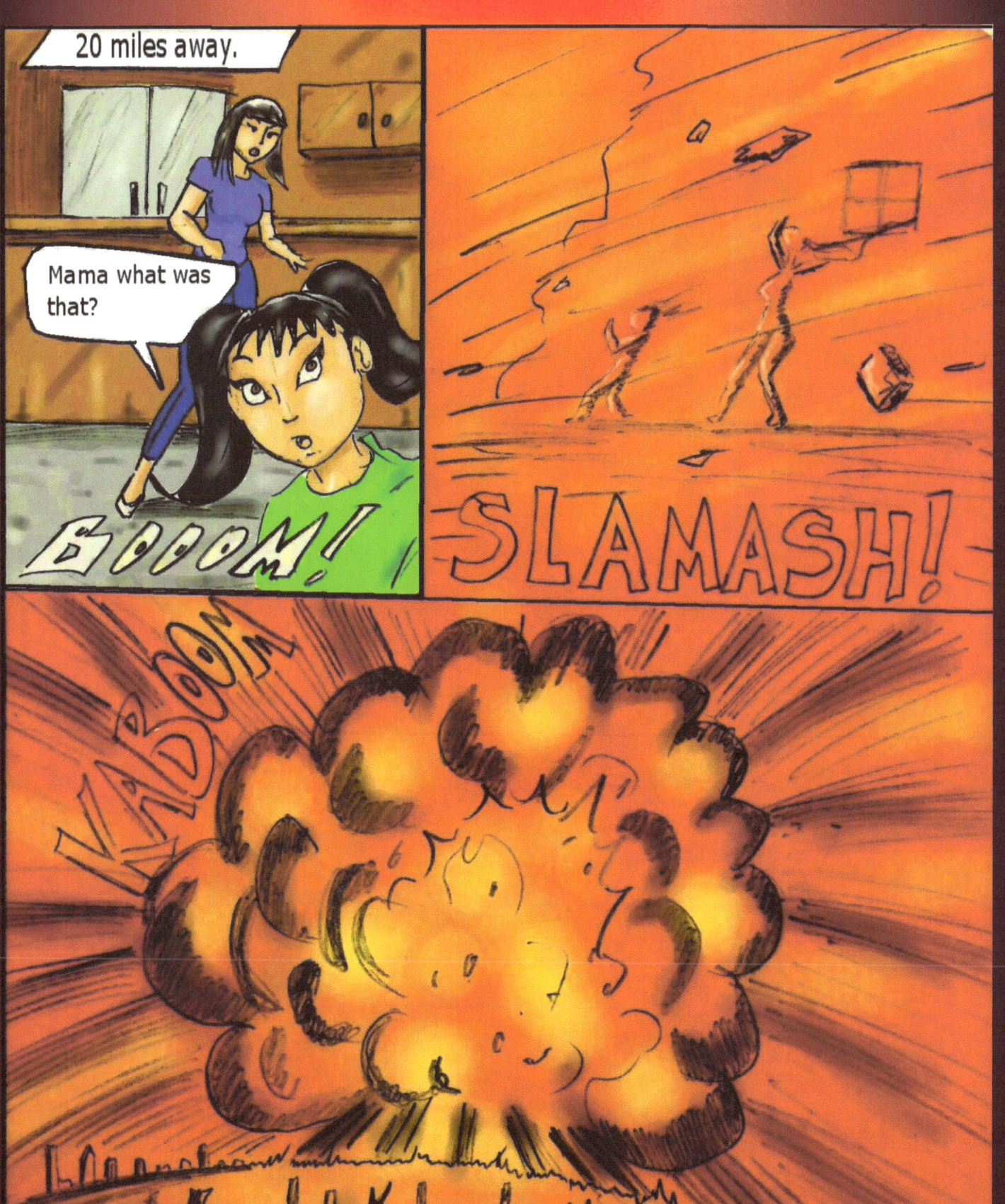

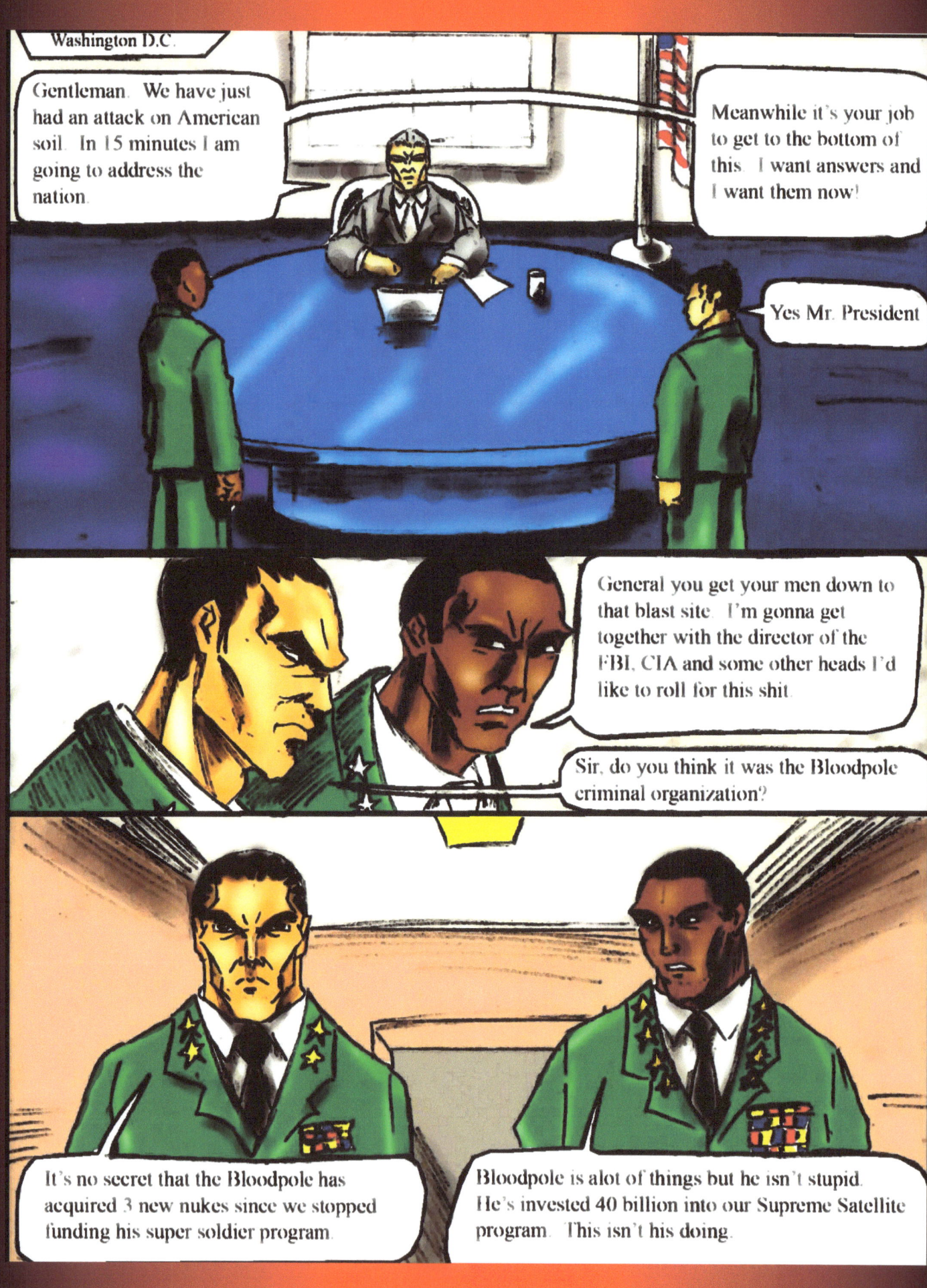

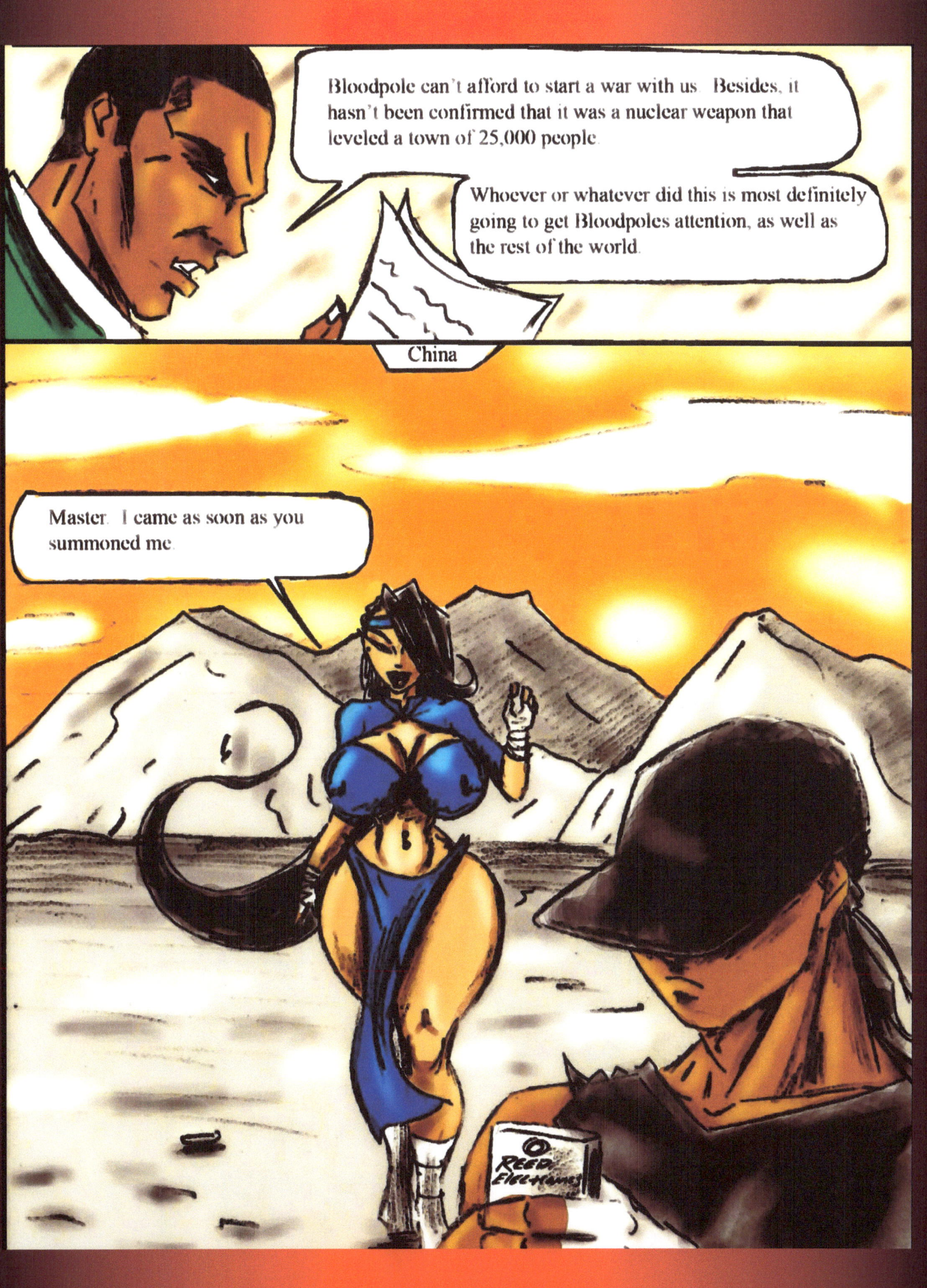

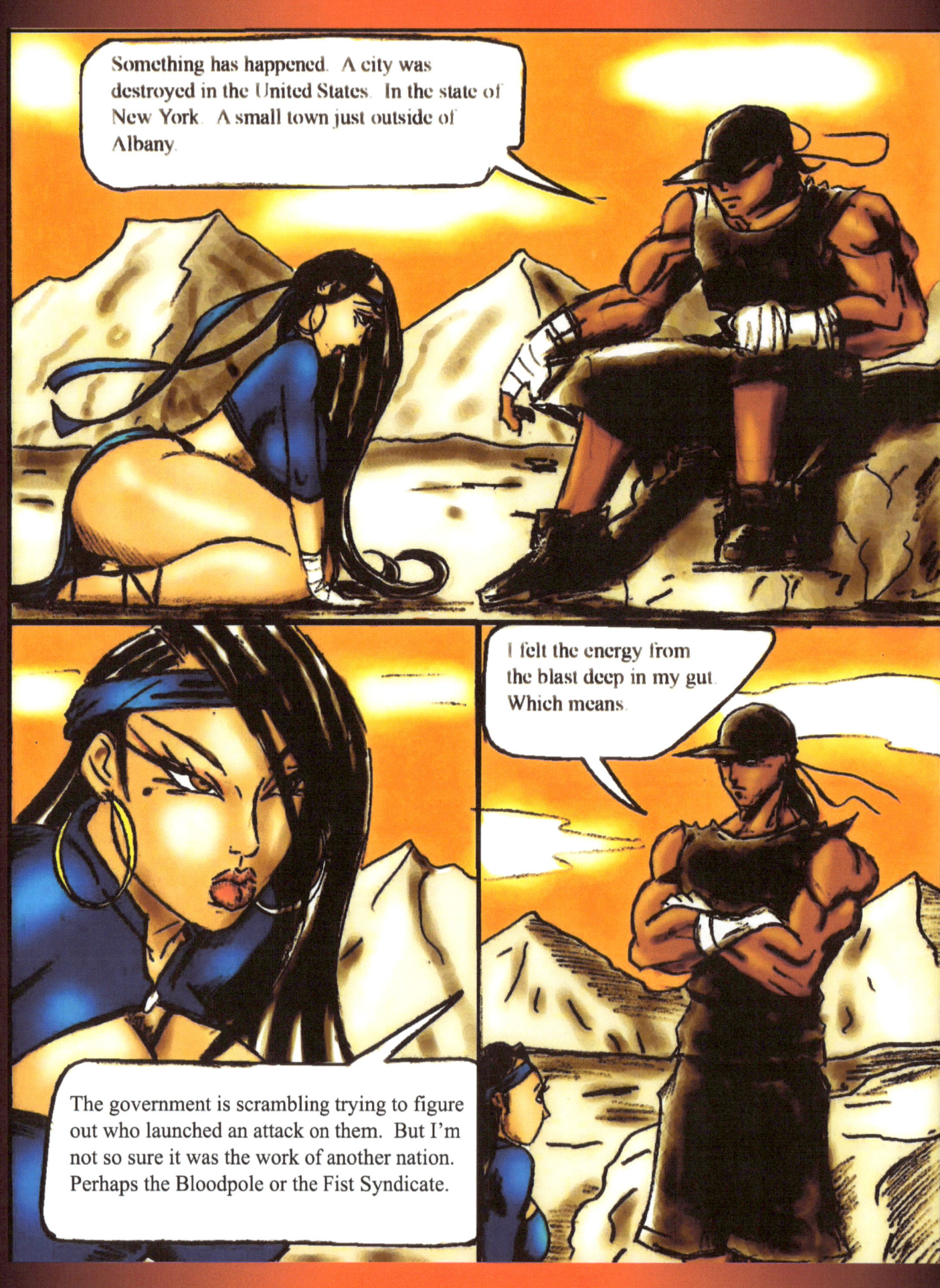

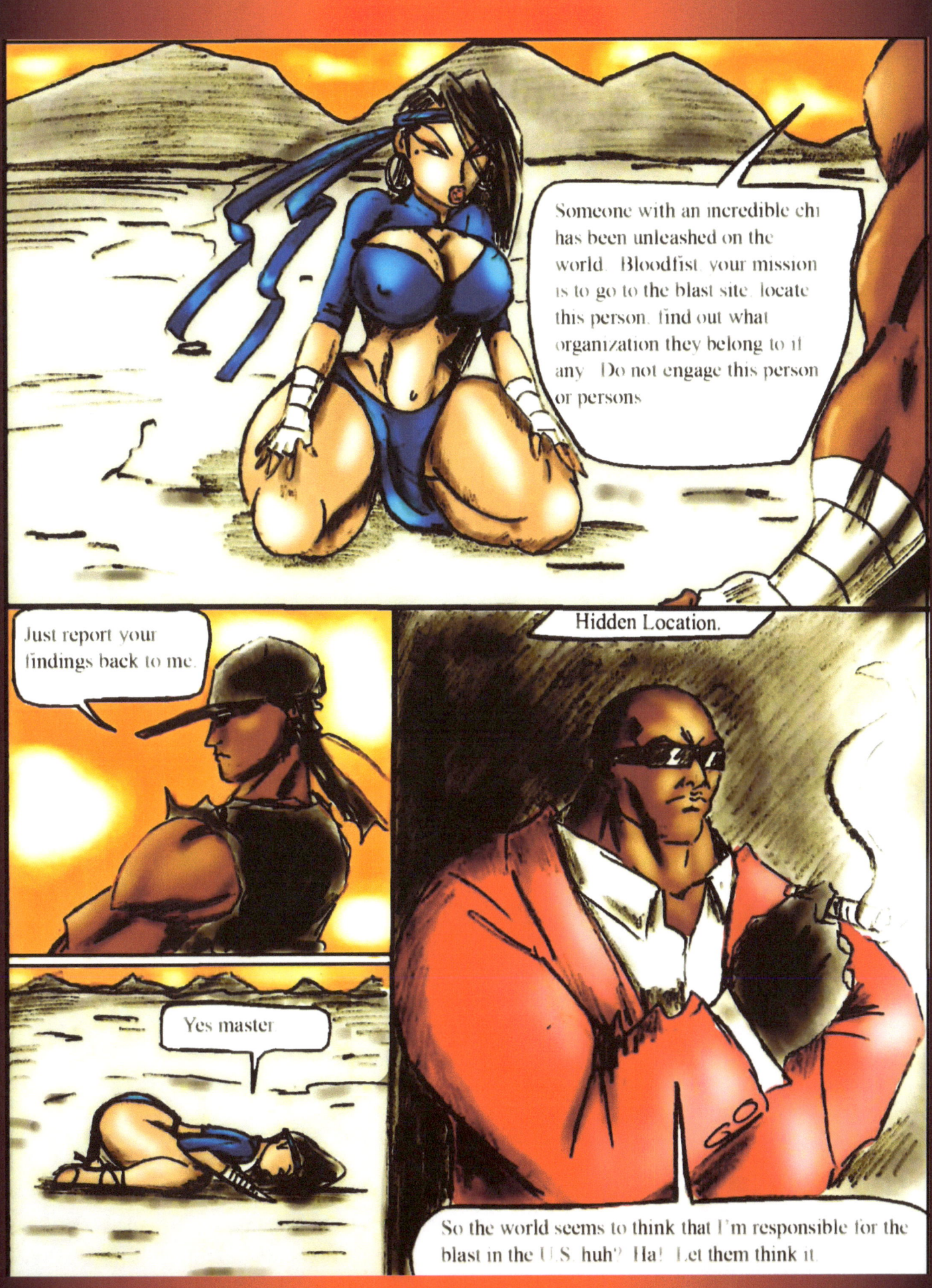

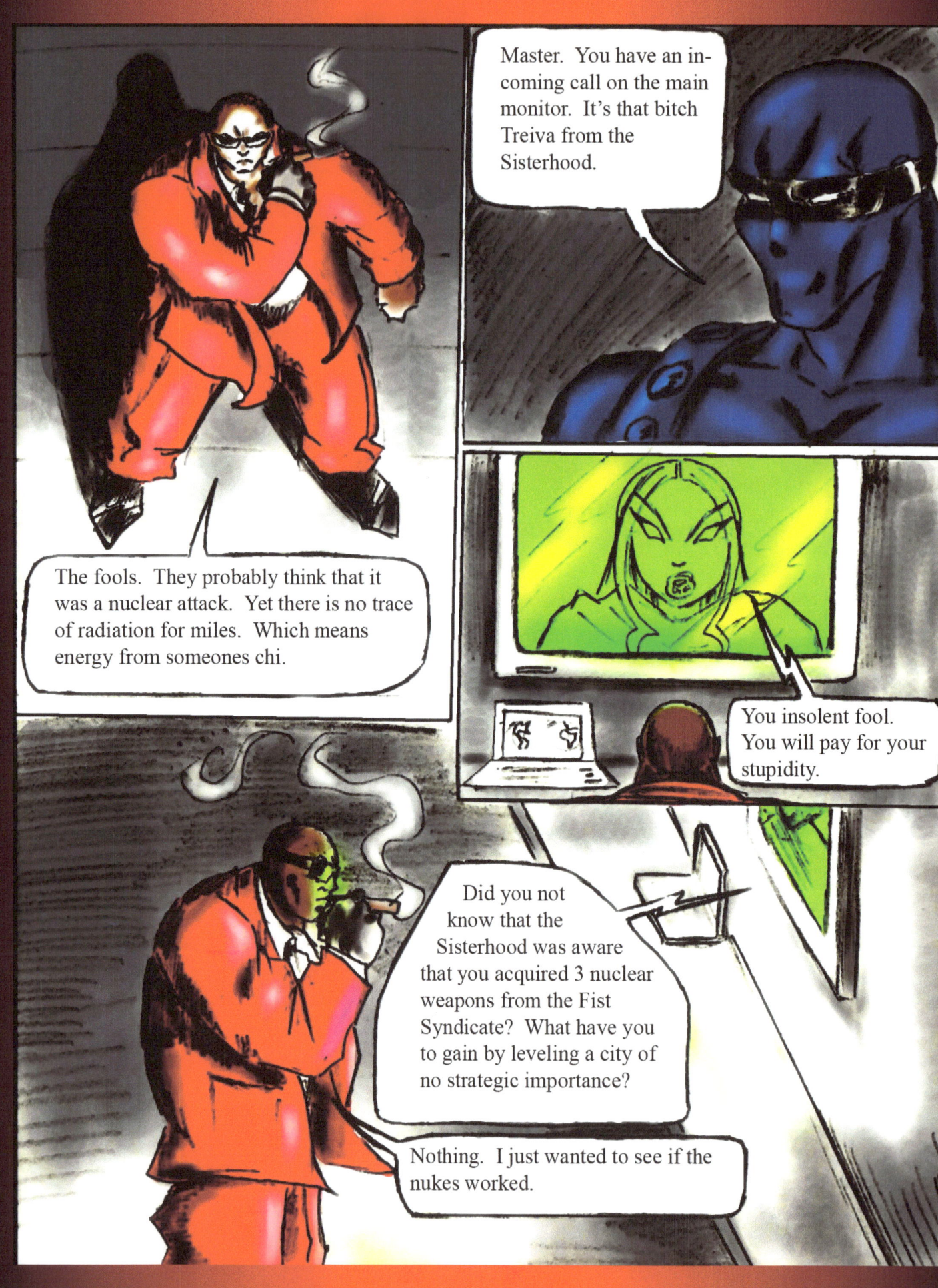

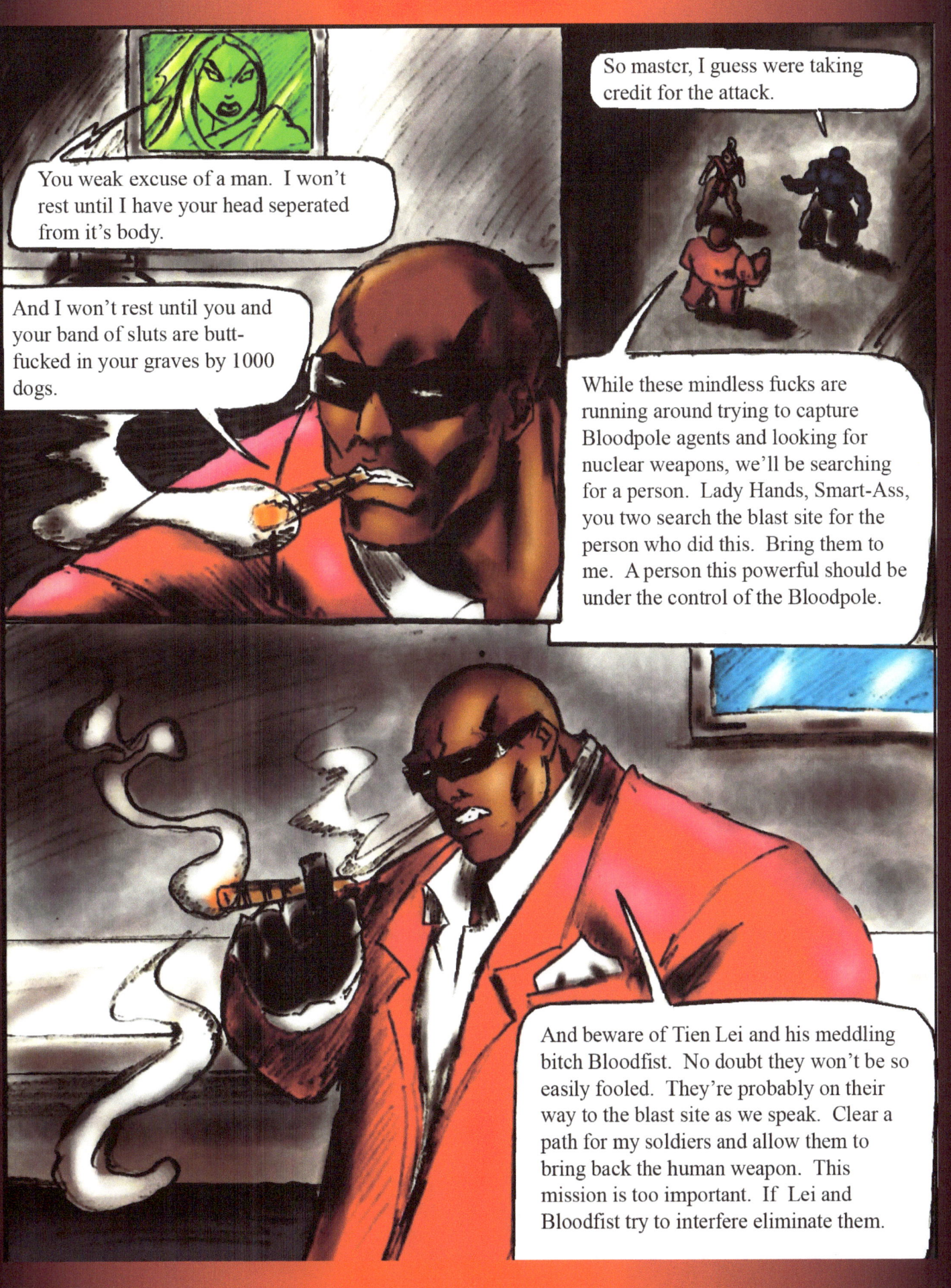

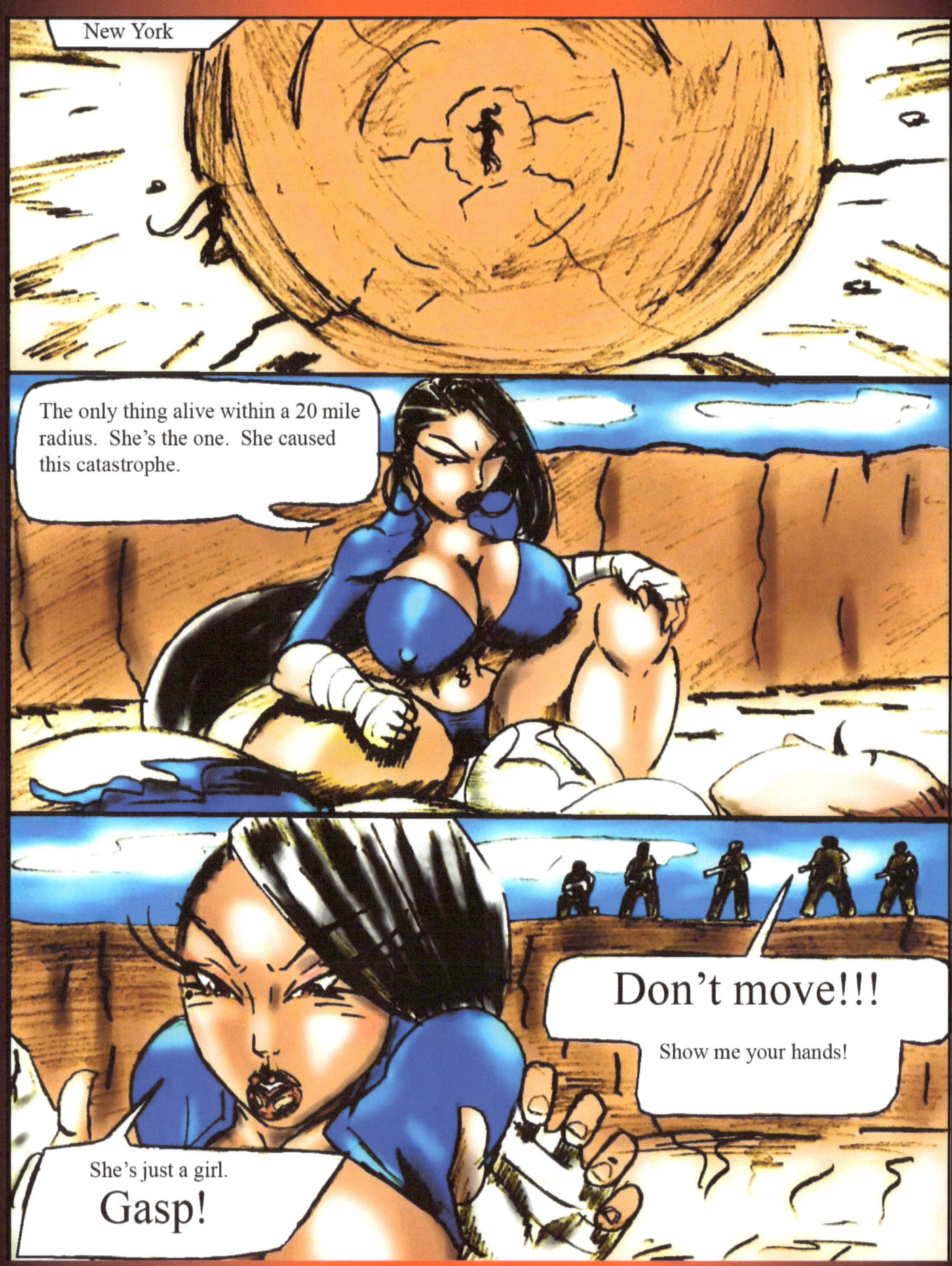

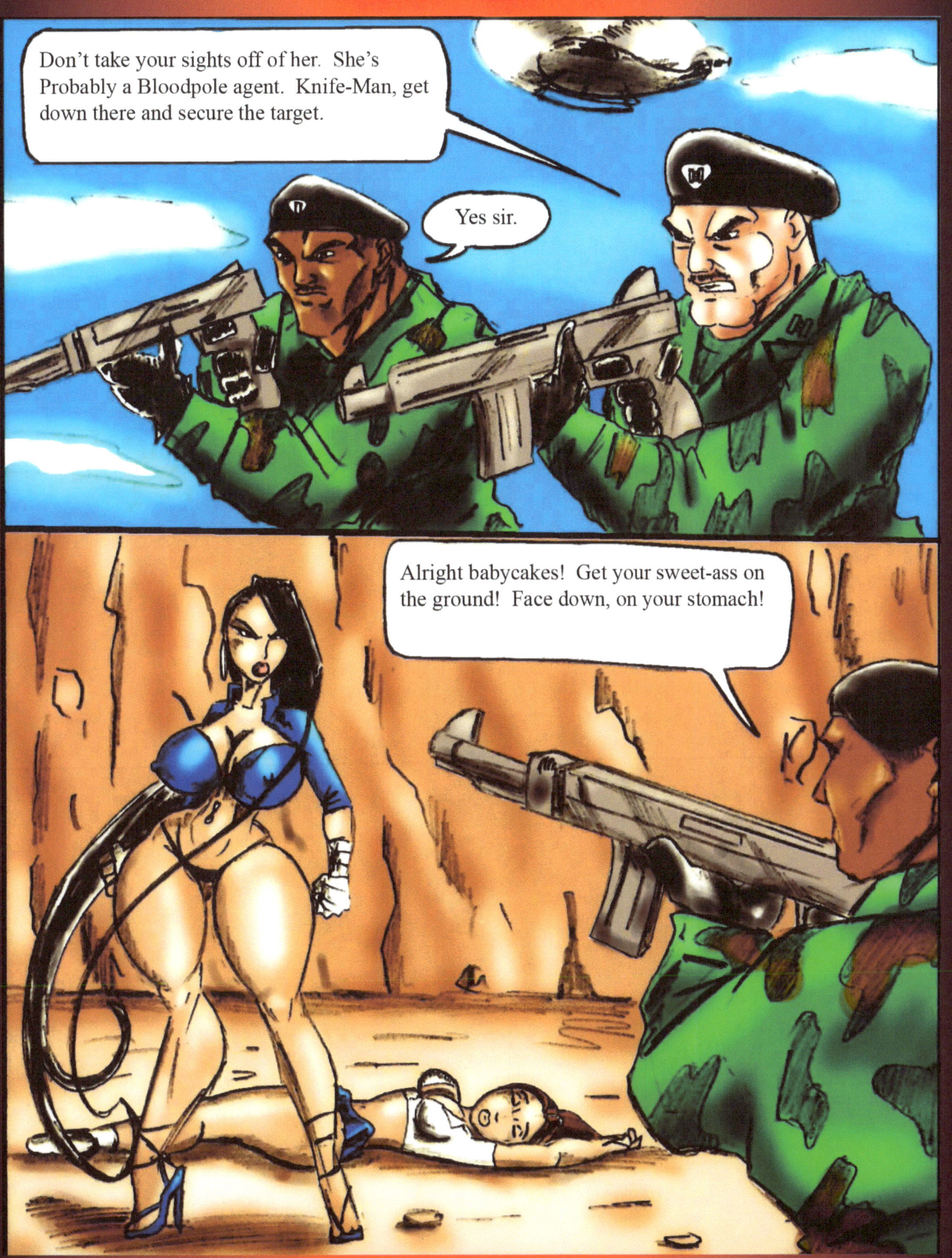

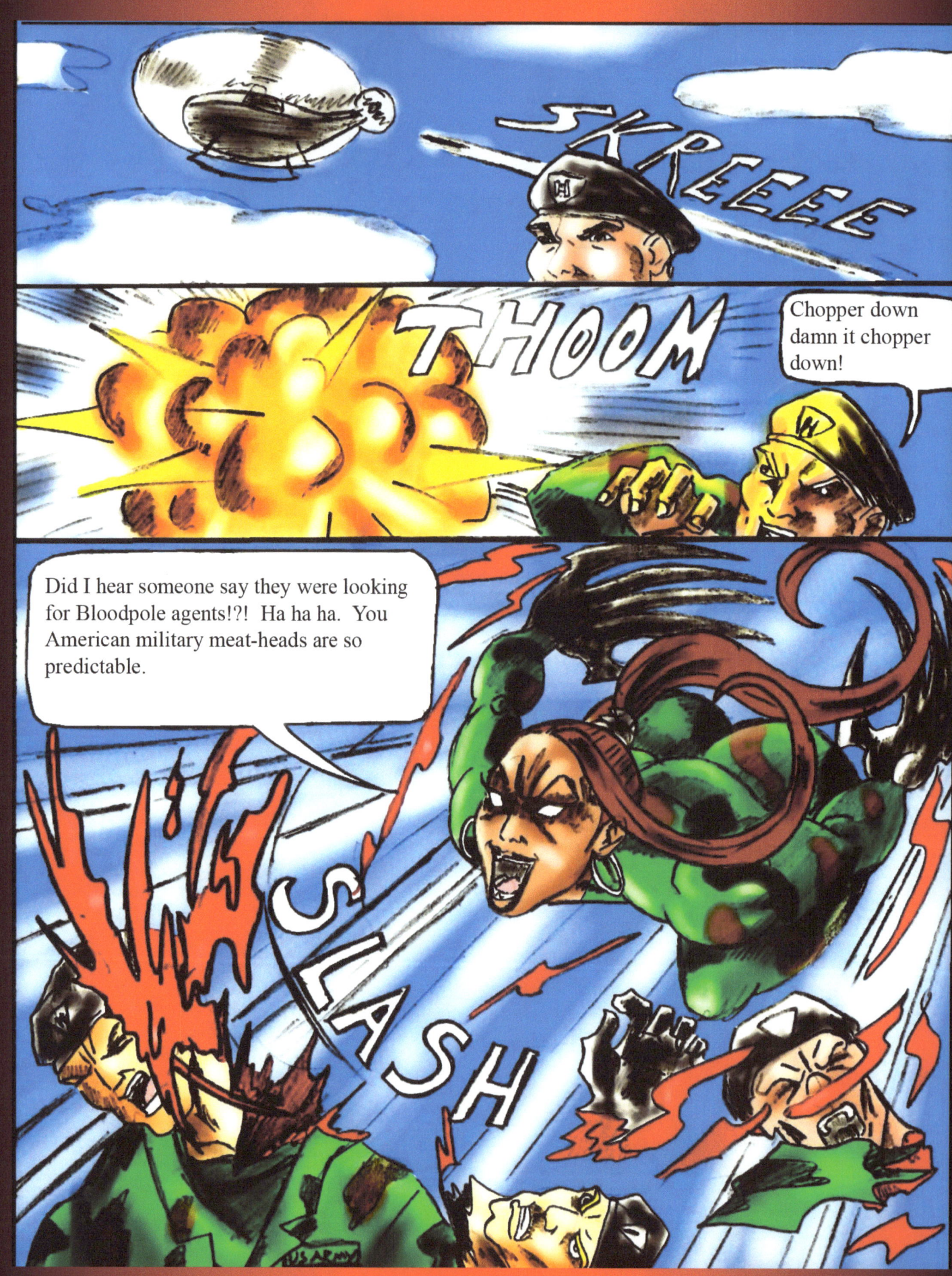

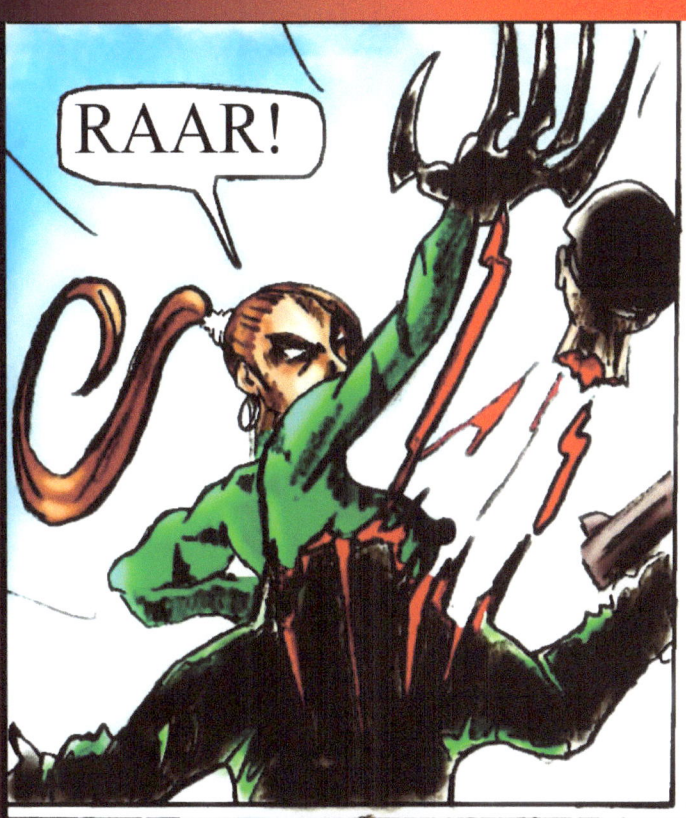

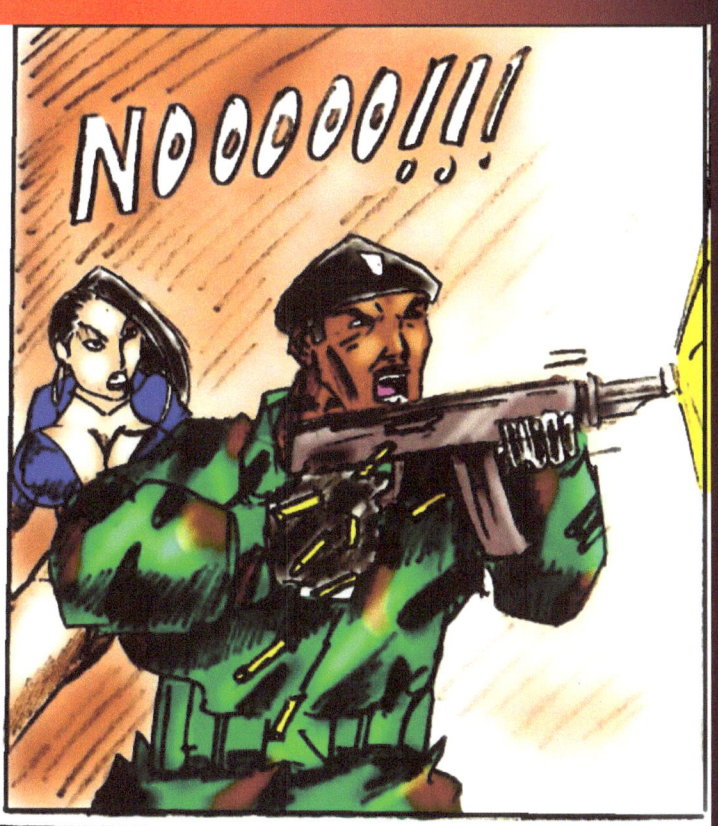

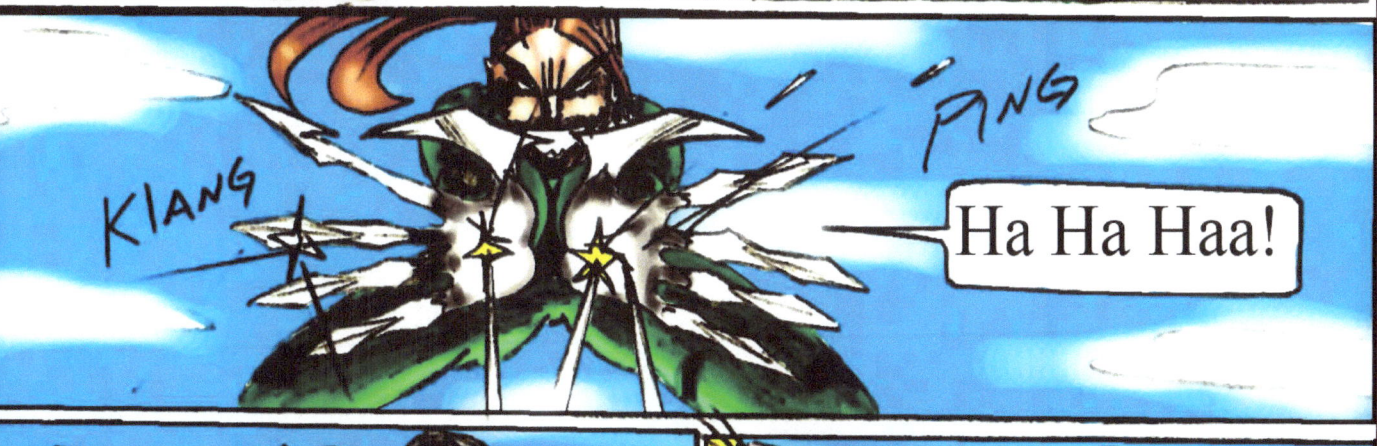

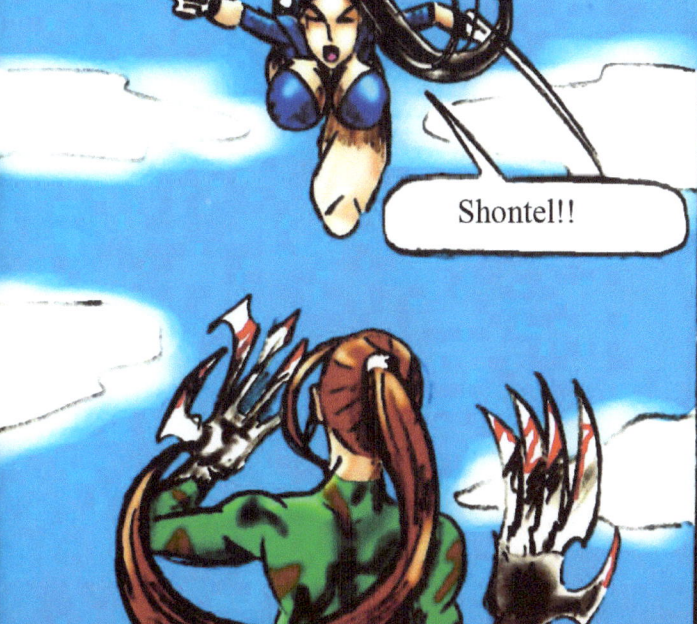

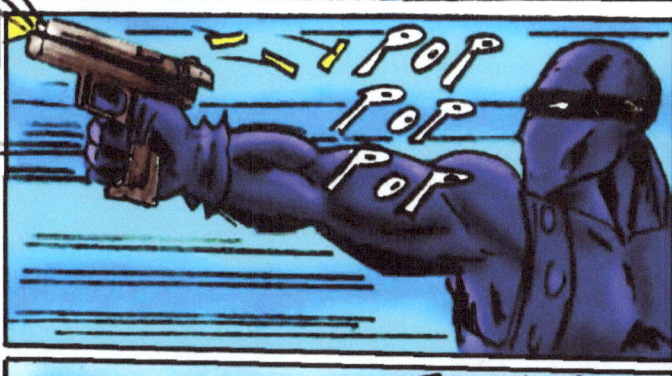

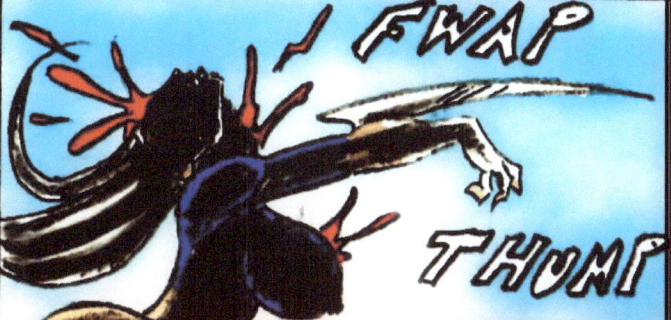

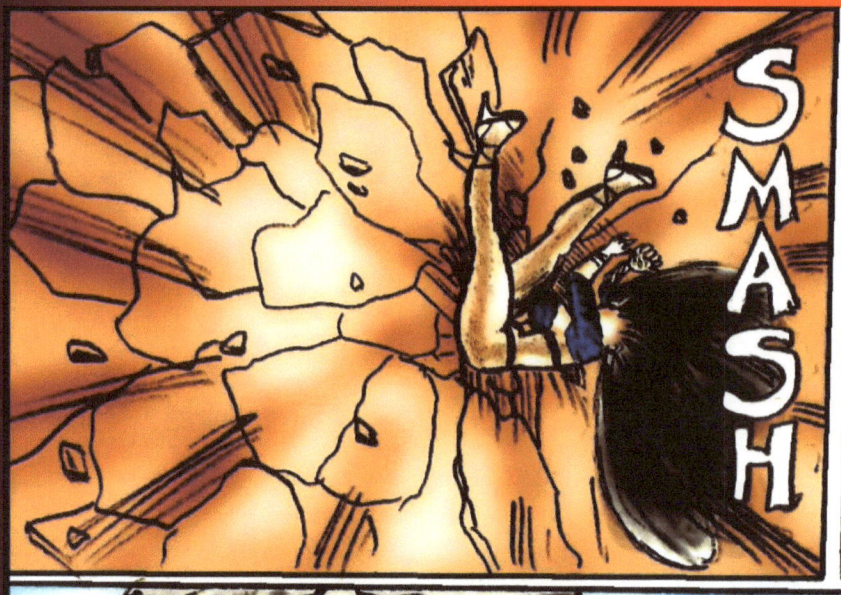

SMASH

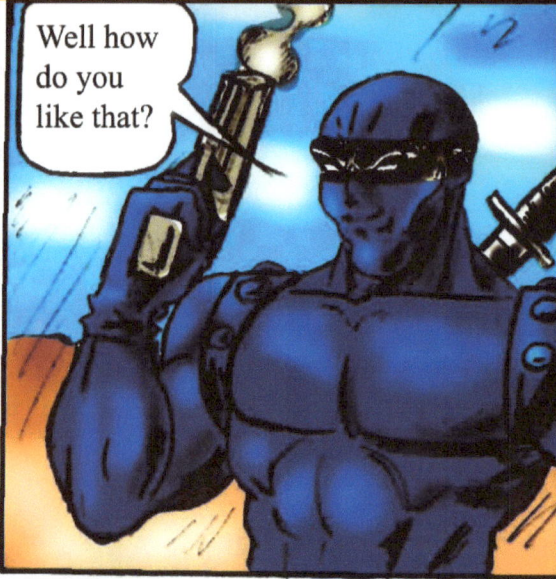

Well how do you like that?

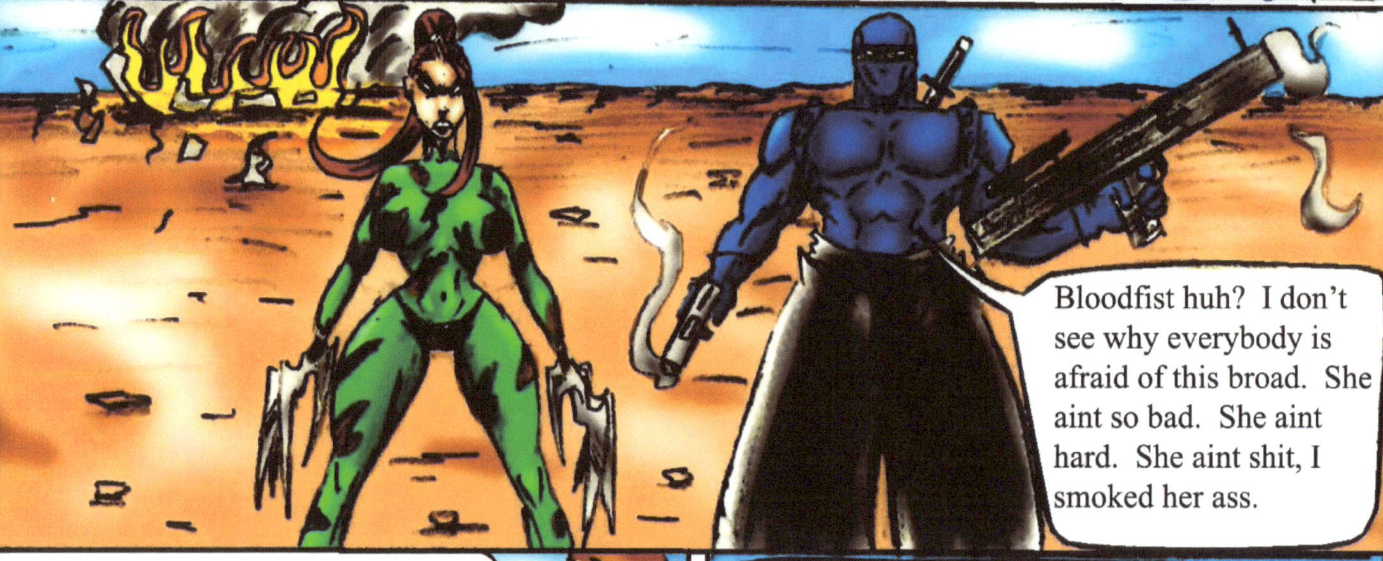

Bloodfist huh? I don't see why everybody is afraid of this broad. She aint so bad. She aint hard. She aint shit, I smoked her ass.

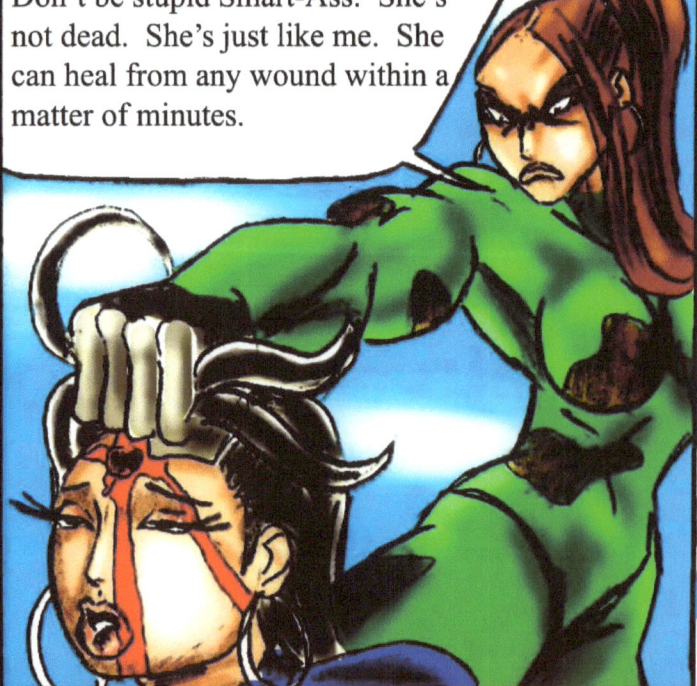

Don't be stupid Smart-Ass. She's not dead. She's just like me. She can heal from any wound within a matter of minutes.

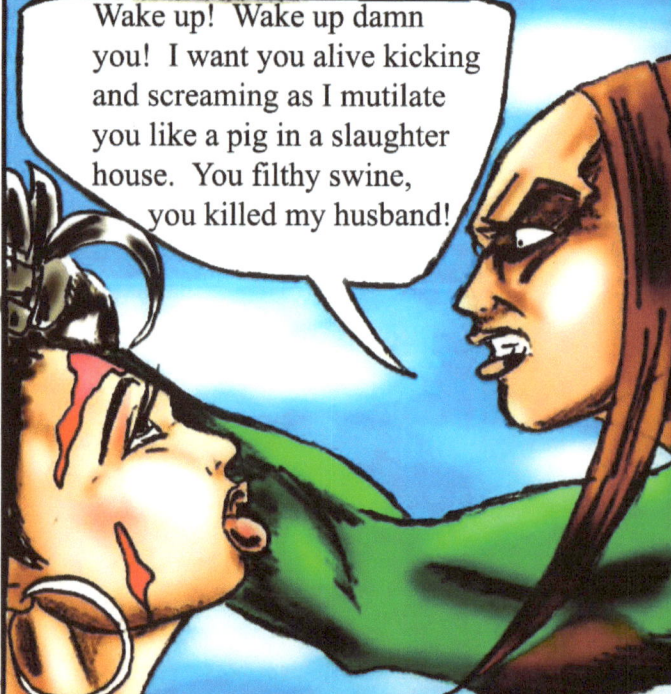

Wake up! Wake up damn you! I want you alive kicking and screaming as I mutilate you like a pig in a slaughter house. You filthy swine, you killed my husband!

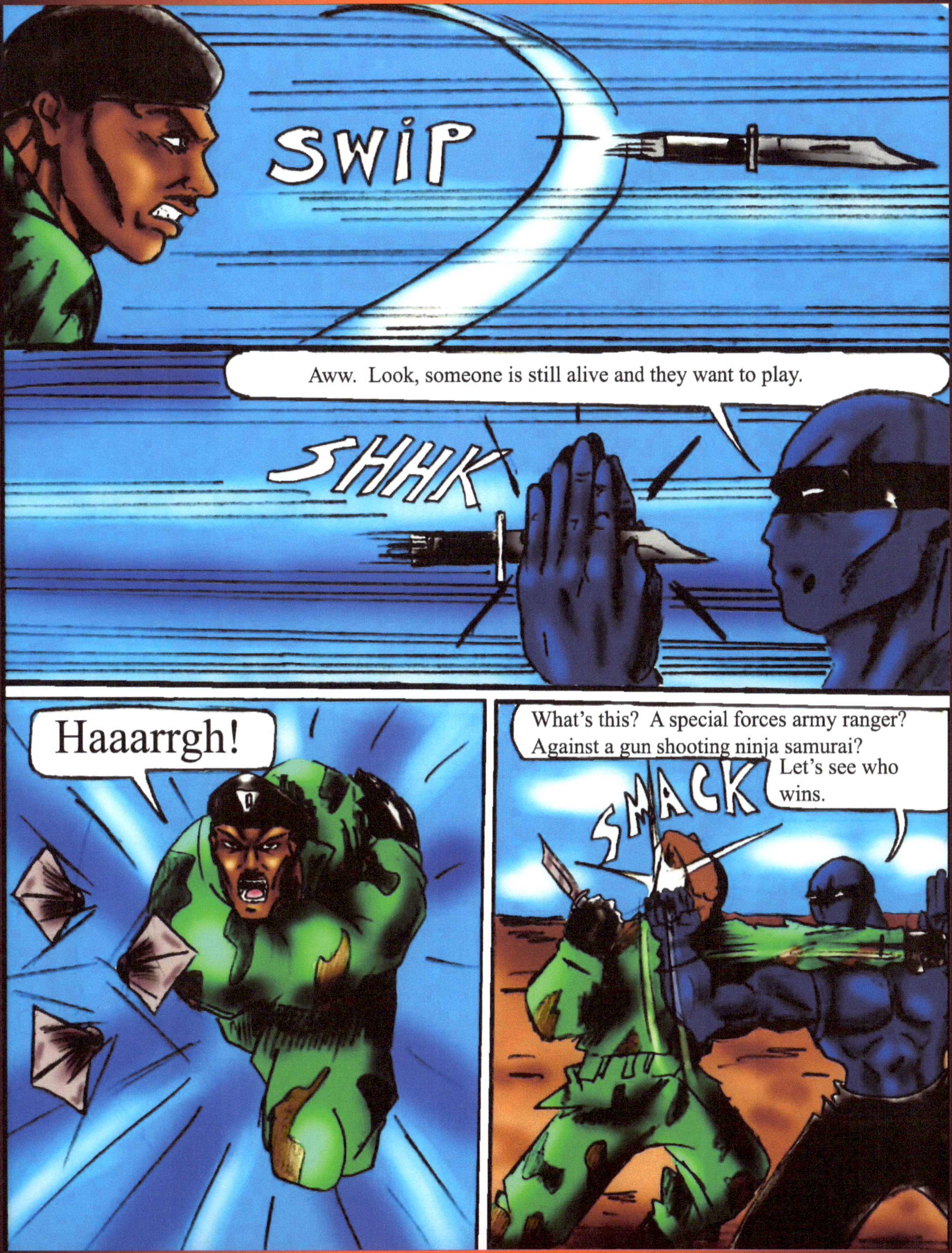

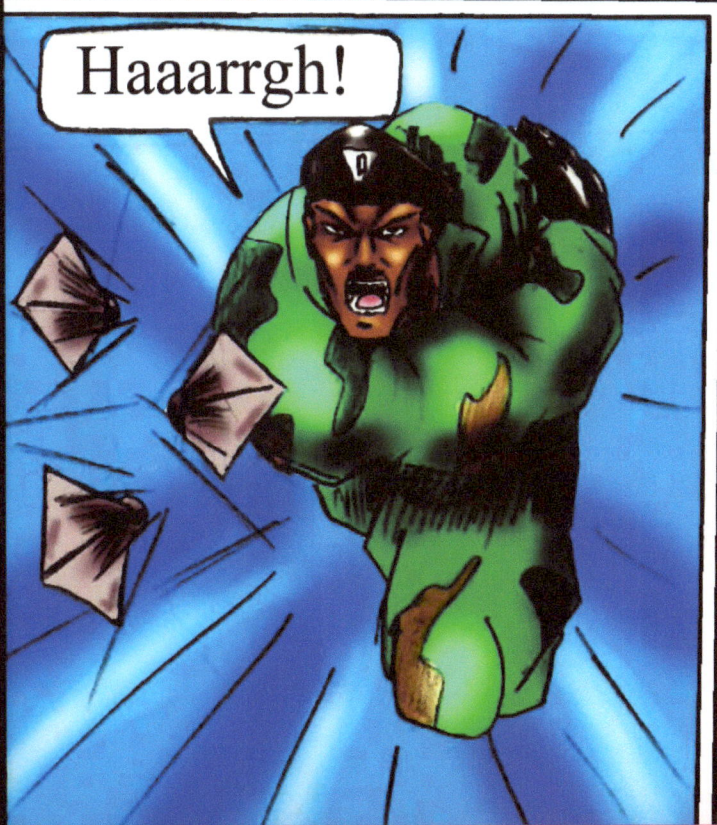
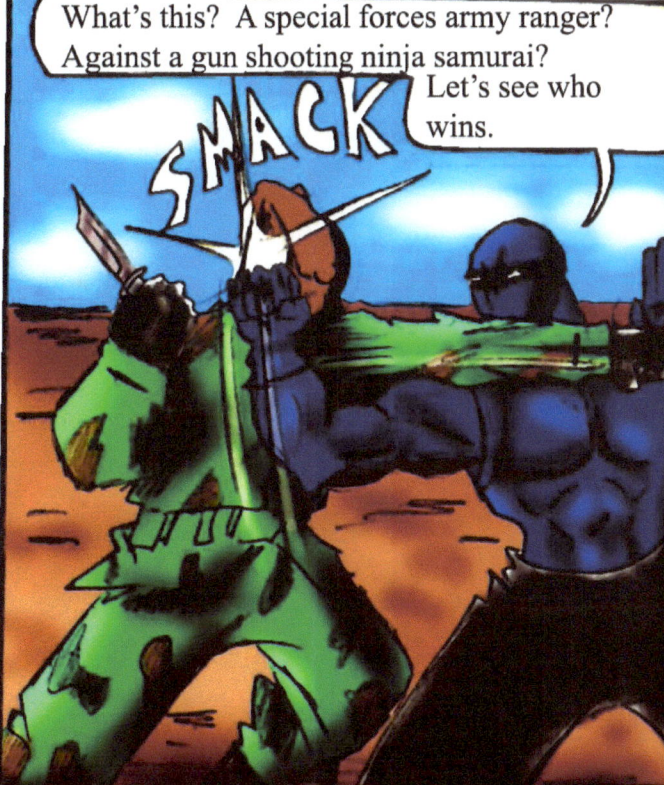

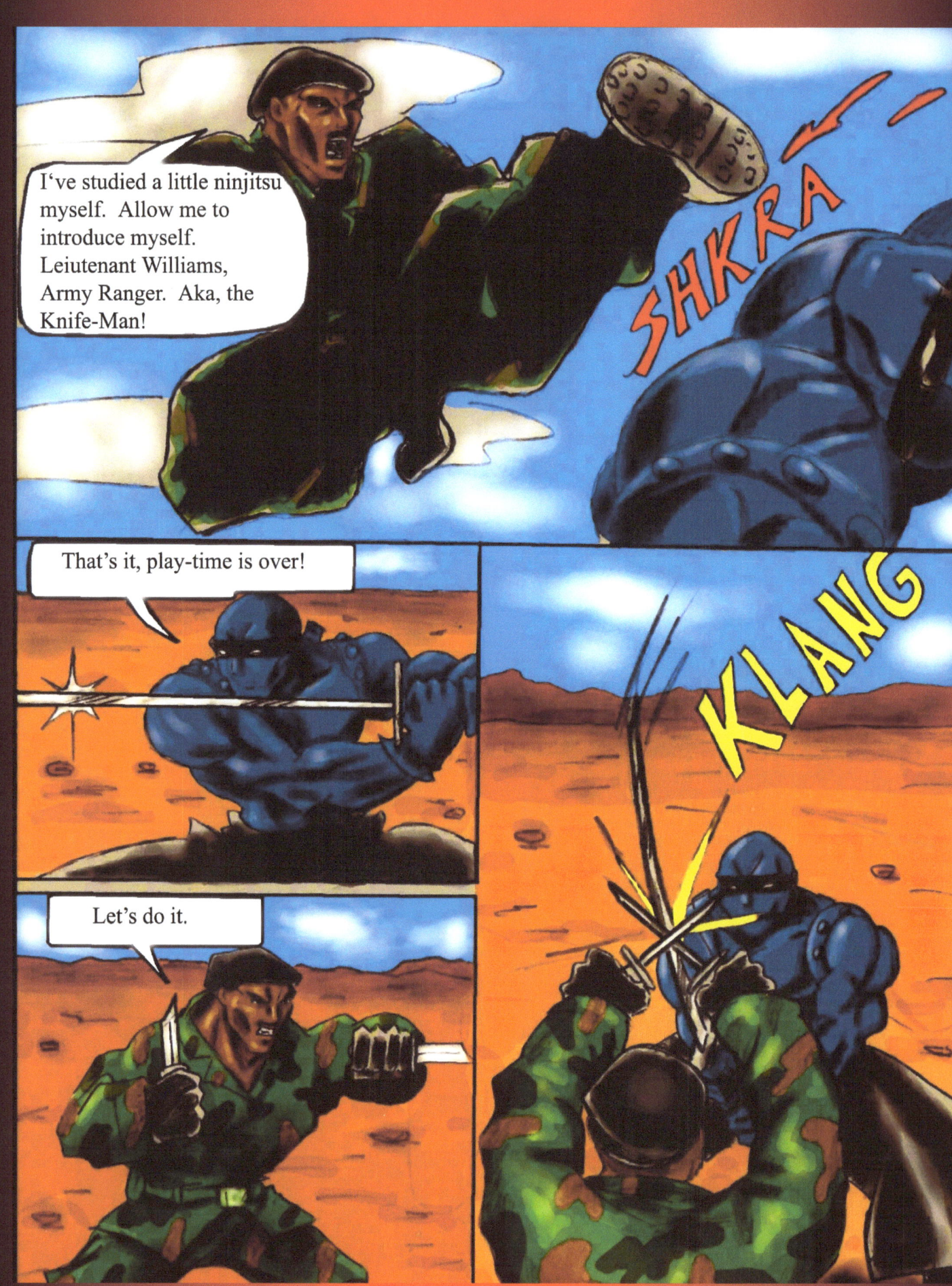

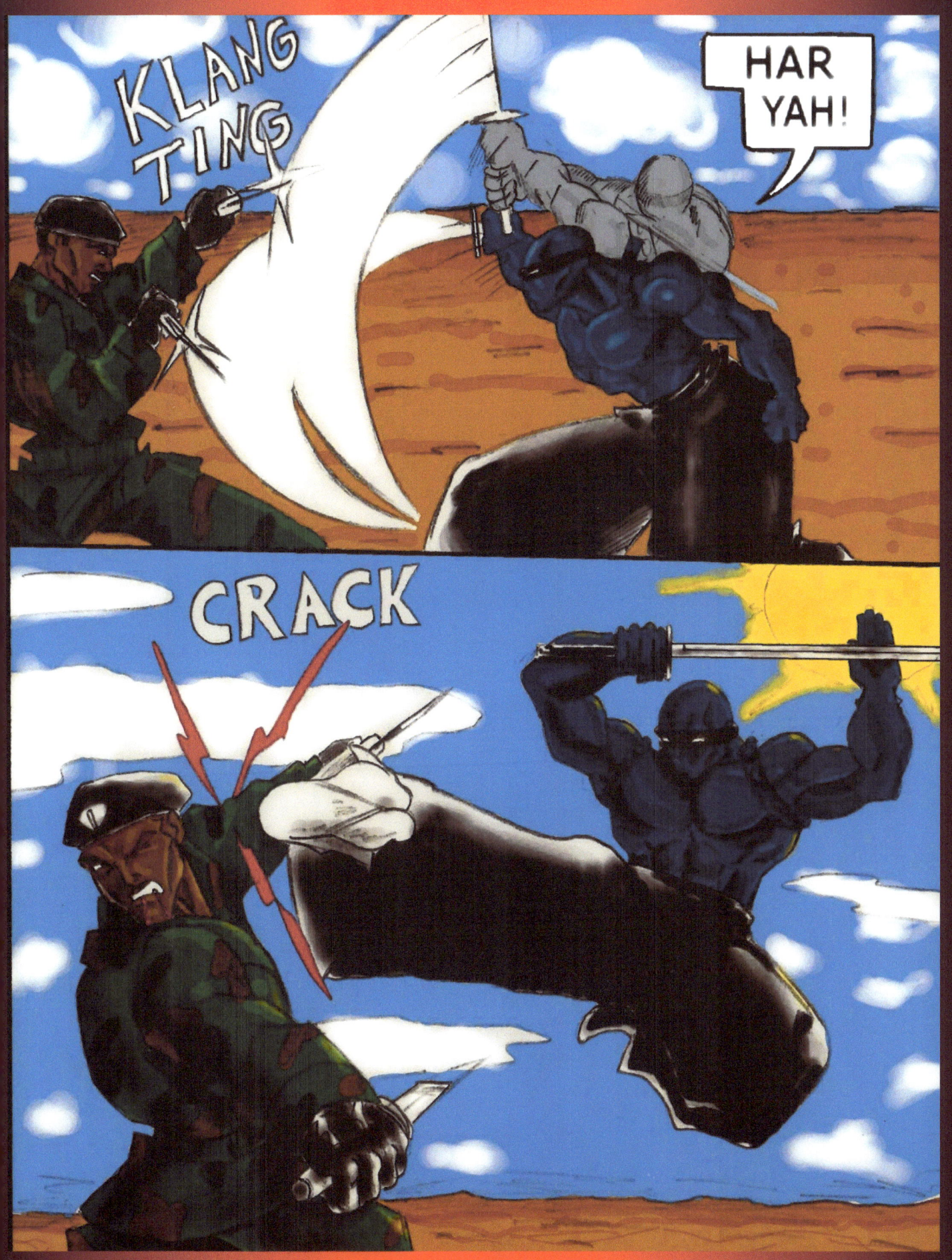

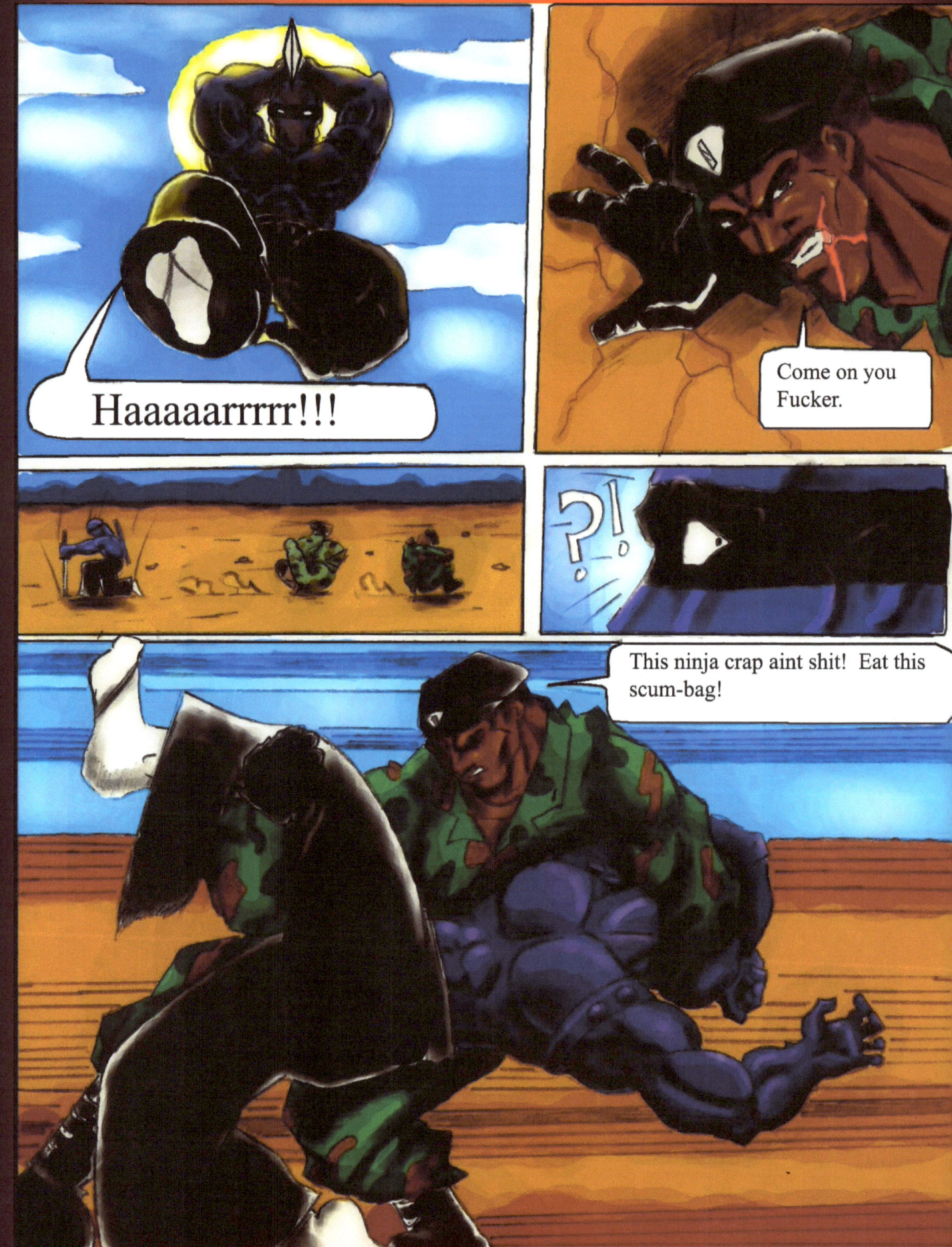

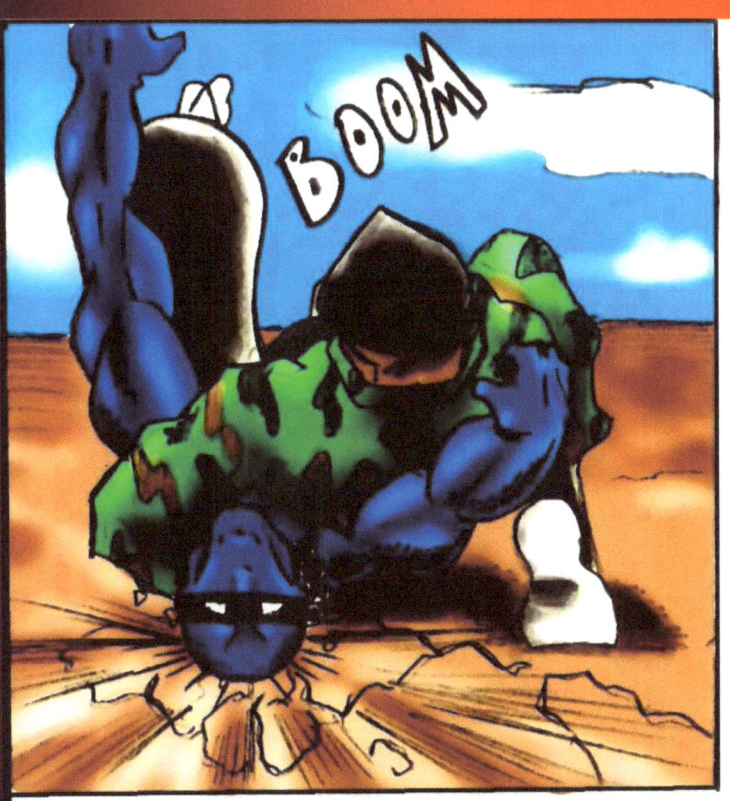

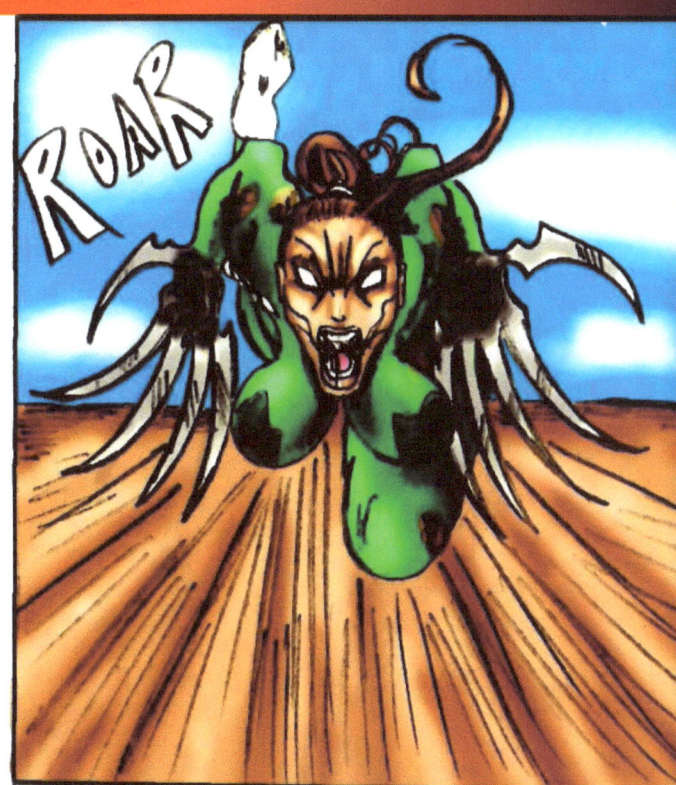

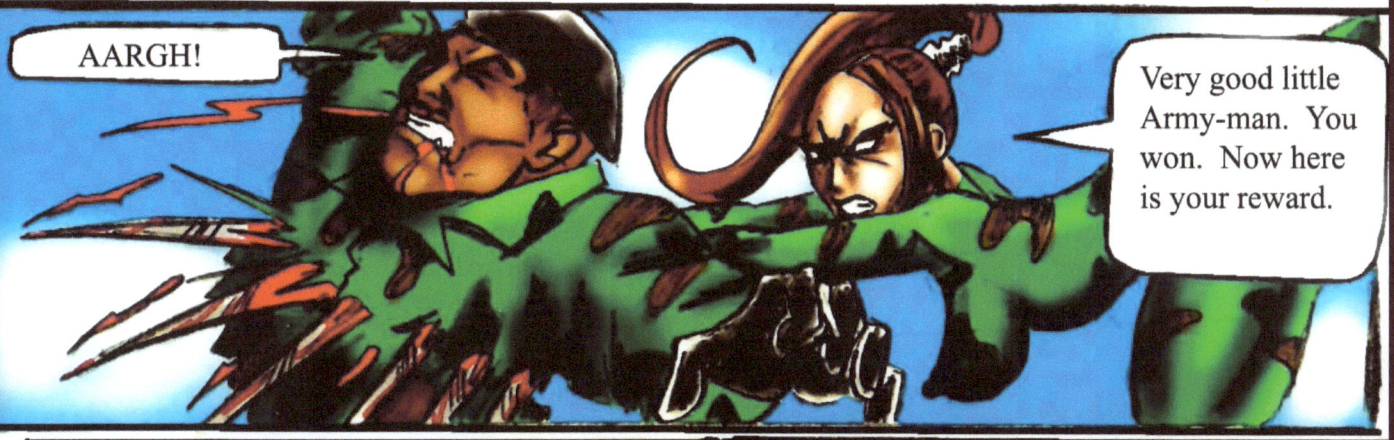

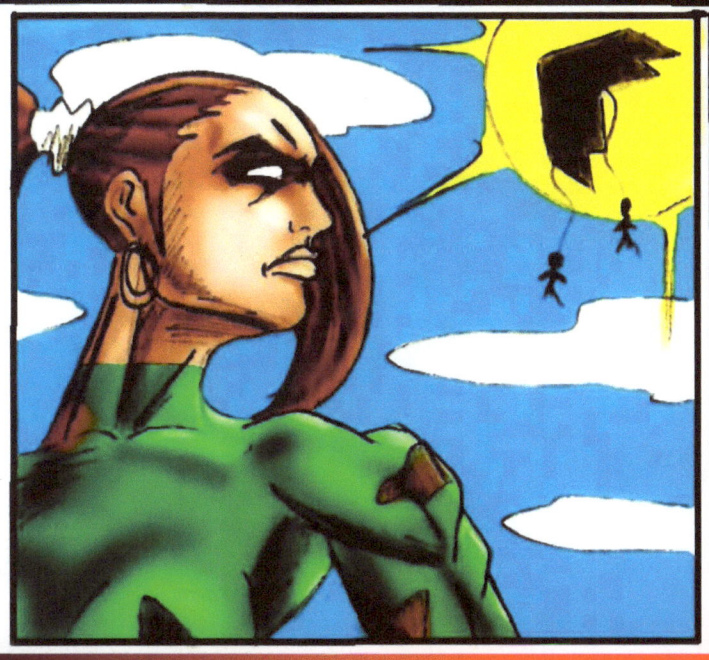

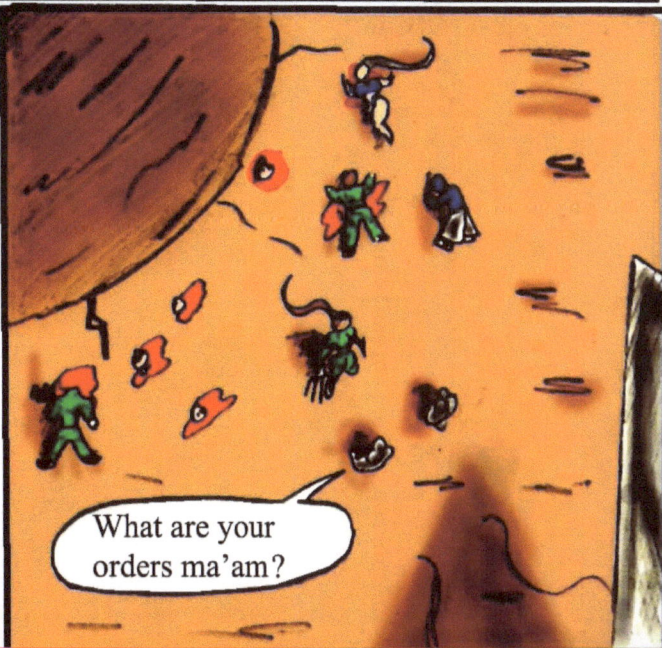

41

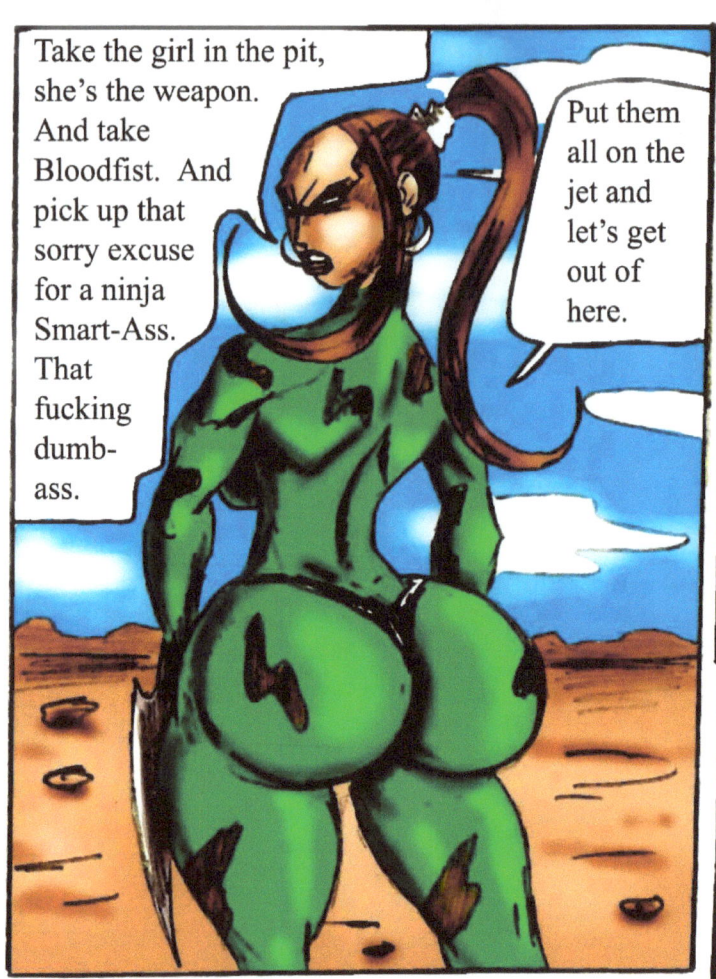

Take the girl in the pit, she's the weapon. And take Bloodfist. And pick up that sorry excuse for a ninja Smart-Ass. That fucking dumb-ass.

Put them all on the jet and let's get out of here.

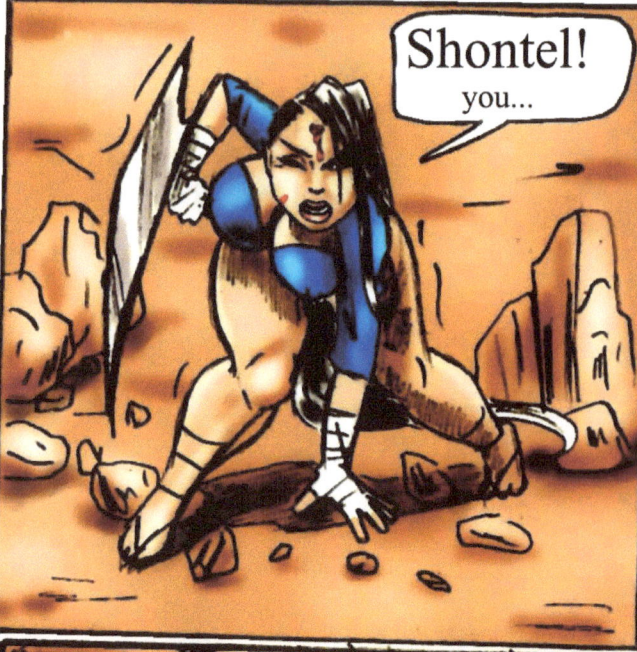

Shontel! you...

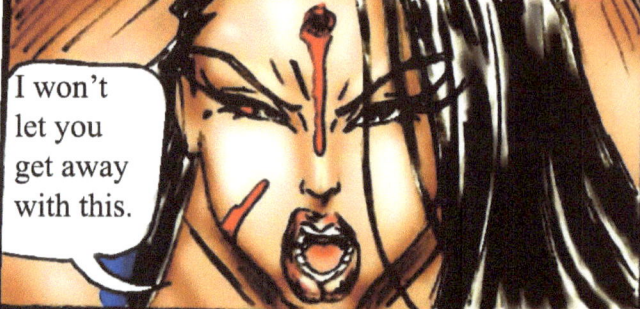

I won't let you get away with this.

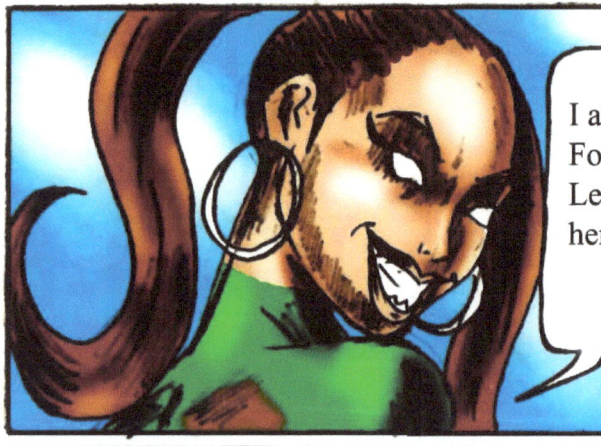

I already have. Forget Bloodfist. Let's get out of here.

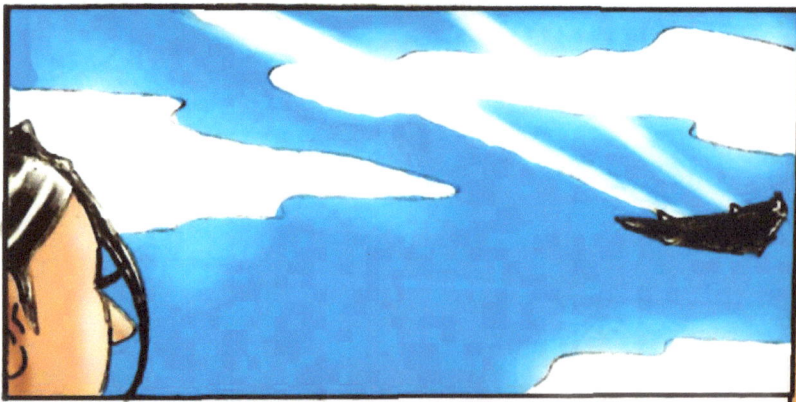

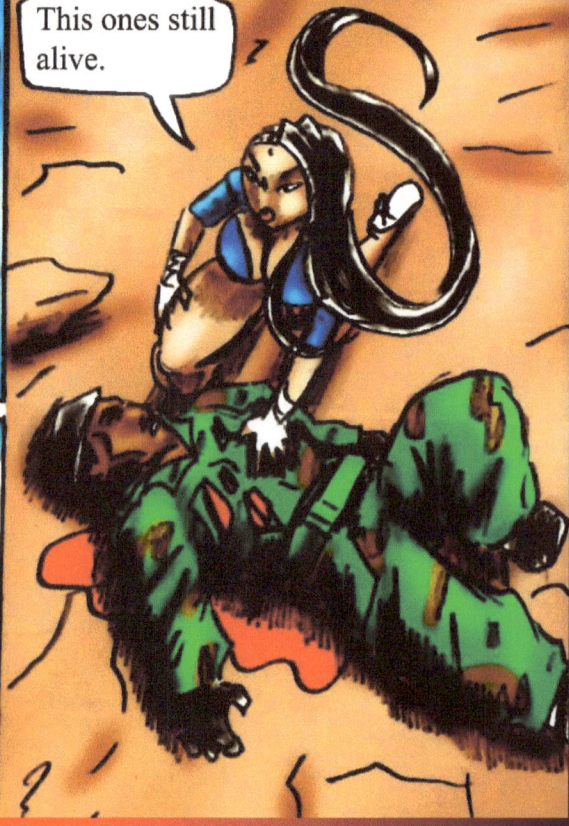

This ones still alive.

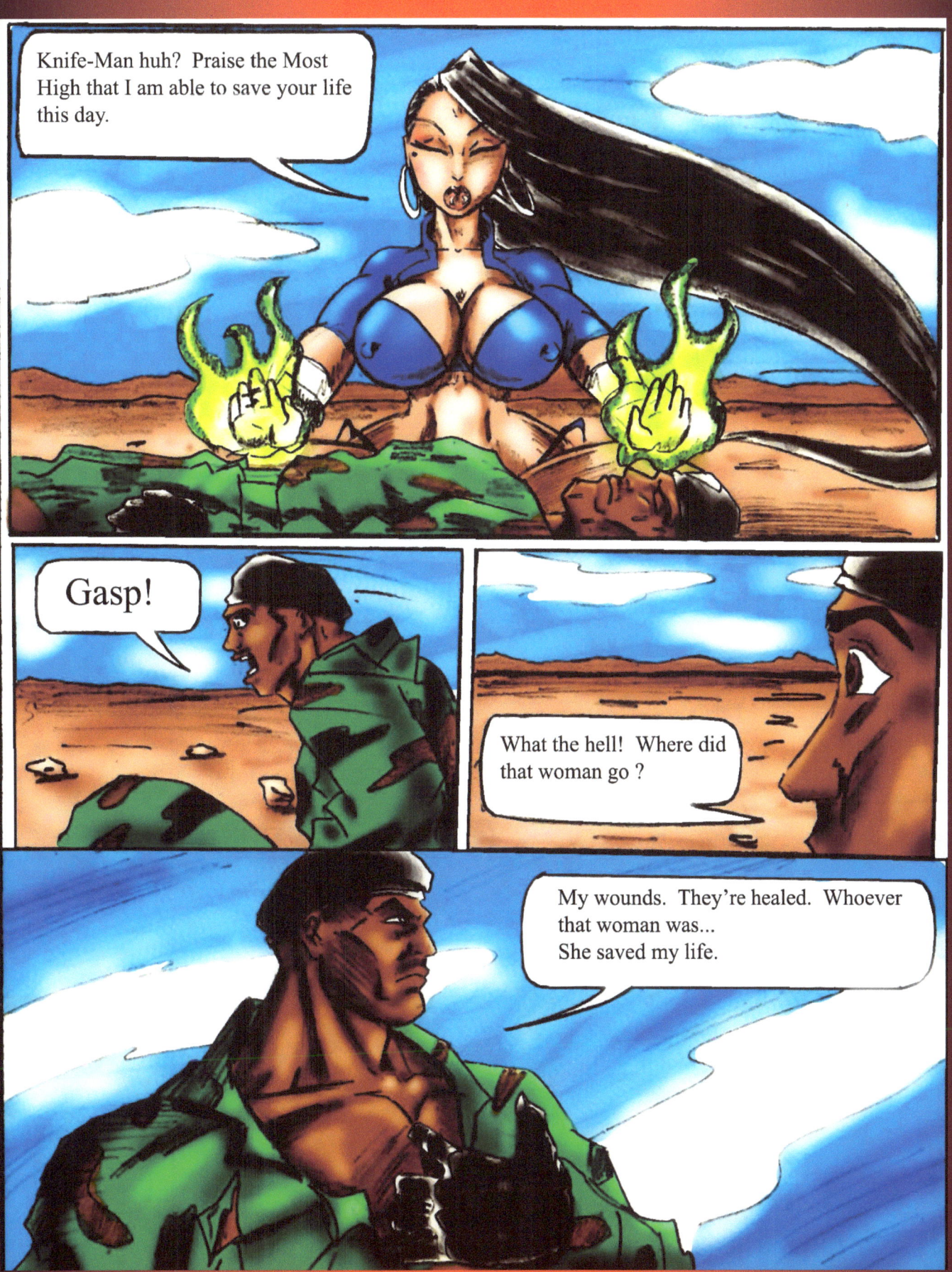

43

Lady Hands

Name: Shontel Chan aka Lady Hands

Born: 1880

Birthplace: Tibet

Height: 5'6"

Weight: 140 lbs.

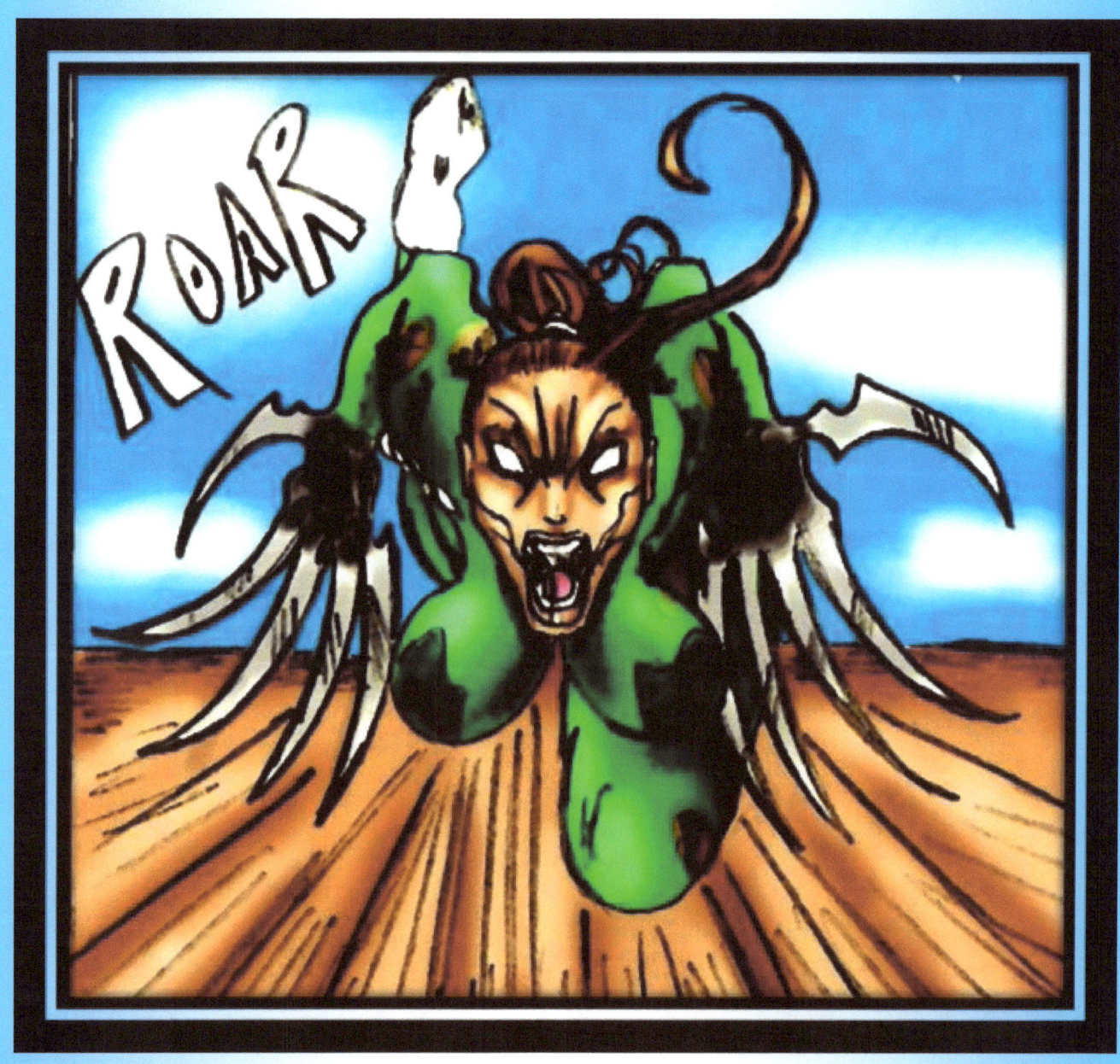

Bio: Not much is known about Shontel's childhood. What is known about her is that she was a scientist who worked side by side with Professor Chan. She was also married to him. Not only was she Professor Chan's wife and one of his scientists, she was also his body guard. When Professor Chan was on the run from the Japanese government for stealing and selling government secrets to Russia, Shontel gave him refuge and helped him regroup and helped him build an organization to take down the Japanese government. Her hatred for the Japanese stemmed from her love and obsession for her husband. She hated whatever he hated. She loved whatever he loved. And he loved nothing but power and control. Together they created a small group of super soldiers to assassinate key generals and politicians in the Japanese government and they would steal their military

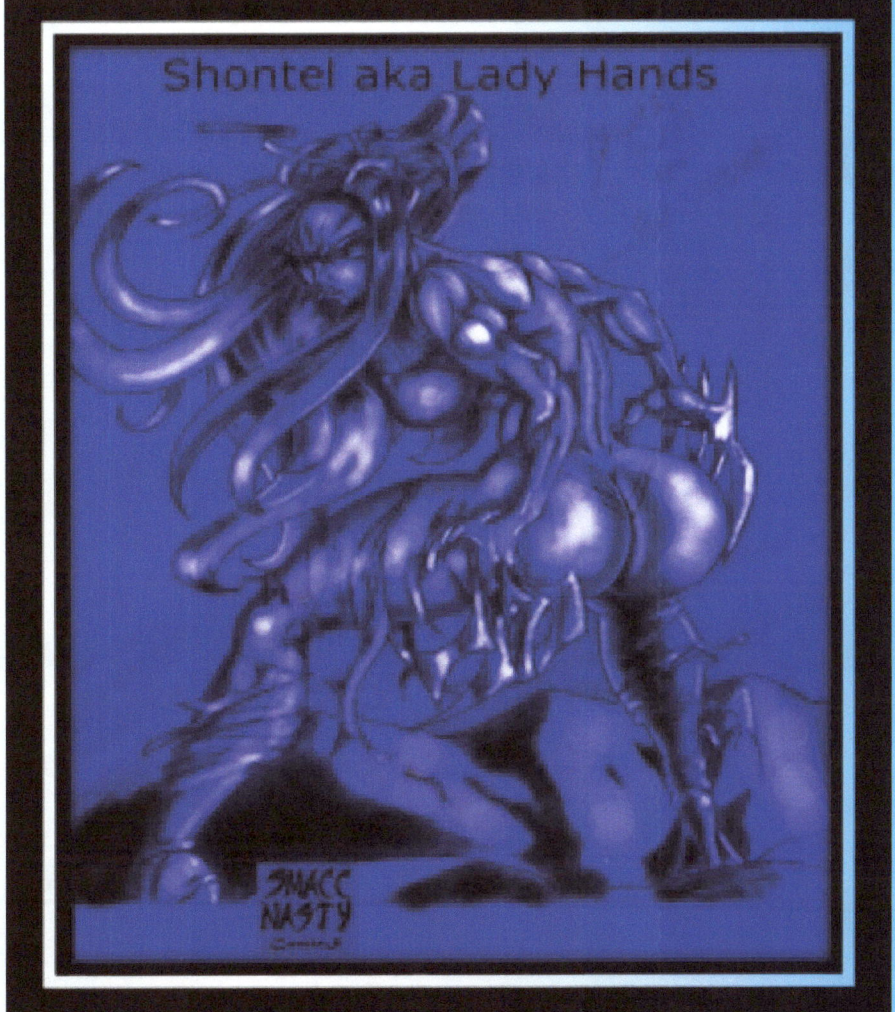

secrets and deliver them to the Russians and the Americans. Professor Chan would do anything to make life hard on the Japanese government. Shontel was somewhat trained in Kung-Fu but she didn't really become a violent and ferocious killer until her husband was killed by one of the subjects that they experimented on, a subject named Bloodfist. After Bloodfist escaped Shontel vowed to avenge her husband's death. She no longer cared about the Japanese, all she wanted was revenge. Shontel took all of her late husband's notes on the project called 'Weapon Claw', the notes that produced the abilities of Bloodfist. Shontel engineered her own body into a living weapon with the help of a man named Bloodpole who was gaining influence in the criminal underworld. Bloodpole taught her to fight and trained her with martial arts experts from around the world. Shontel trained day and night for 70 years obsessing over her husband's death. Finally in late 2000, Bloodpole unleashed his weapon that he named Lady Hands on the world. Lady Hands was the perfect weapon. She could heal from any wound

She could heal from any wound within minutes; she had the strength of a bull and the speed of a leopard. She also had Professor Chan's design for the liquid metal flowing in her hands. She can turn her hands into metal or extend her fingers into razor sharp metal blades. And her healing abilities stop her aging process. Lady Hands is a psychotic killing machine who only thinks of one thing when she fights; killing Bloodfist.

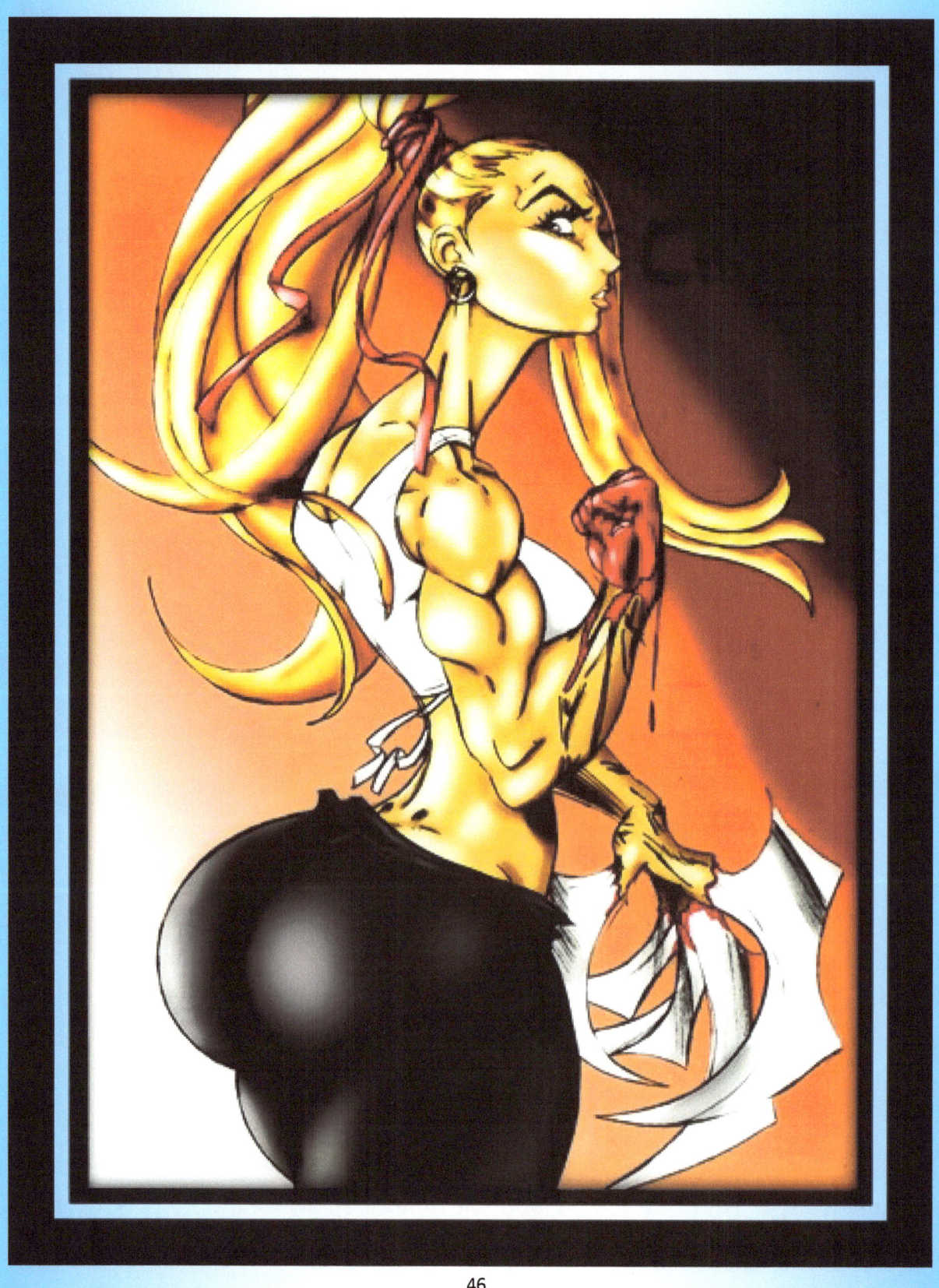

Tien Li aka YeshaYahu

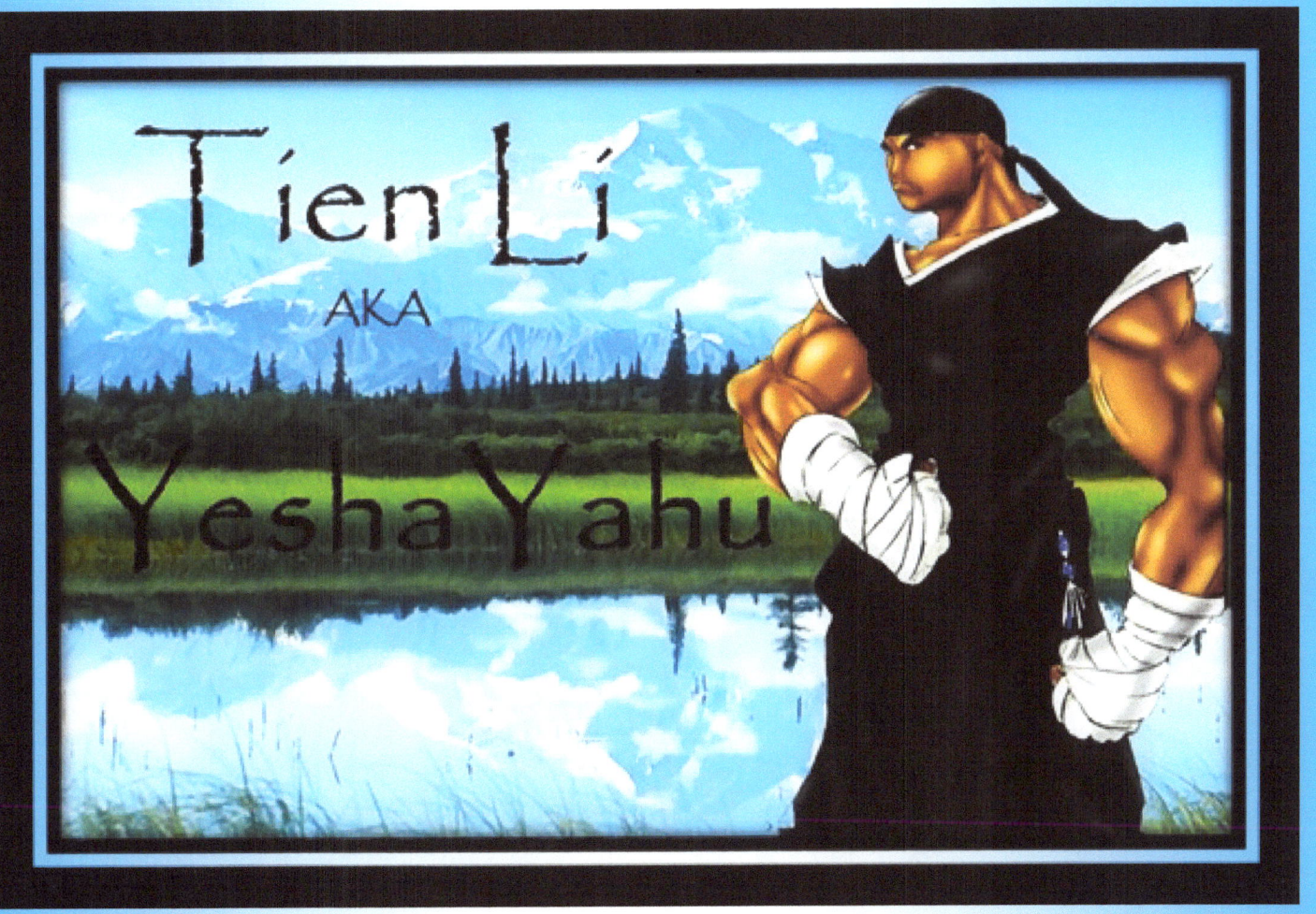

Name: Tien Lei aka YeshaYahu Ben Yisrael

Born: 1849

Birth place: Aksum Ethiopia

Tien Lei was born in Ethiopia. Tien's family was on the run from Arab and European slave traders. After being on the run for years, Tien and his grandfather were taken captive aboard a slave ship. The slaves revolted on the ship and diverted its course at sea and ended up crashing on to the shores of Japan. Tien and his grandfather found refuge with an old samurai master. Tien's grandfather was a master Nuba wrestler and a descendant of the family line of YeshaYahu the prophet. Tien learned to fight from his grandfather and the old samurai

master, developing his own style and turning it into the most deadliest of all forms of martial arts. Tien's grandfather made him commit to memory the scroll of YeshaYahu the prophet for it was the only history of the Sacred Scrolls that the grandfather could remember after being traumatized by the harsh conditions of being on the run.

One day Tien's grandfather fought a battle against the demon Legion-Gog, who sought to drag them back into slavery or kill them. The grandfather was killed in the battle, but the young Tien escaped. Tien Lei vowed revenge. He continued to grow and train under the old samurai who later died of old age a few years later, leaving his entire estate to Tien Lei. Tien, being a young rich master, lives

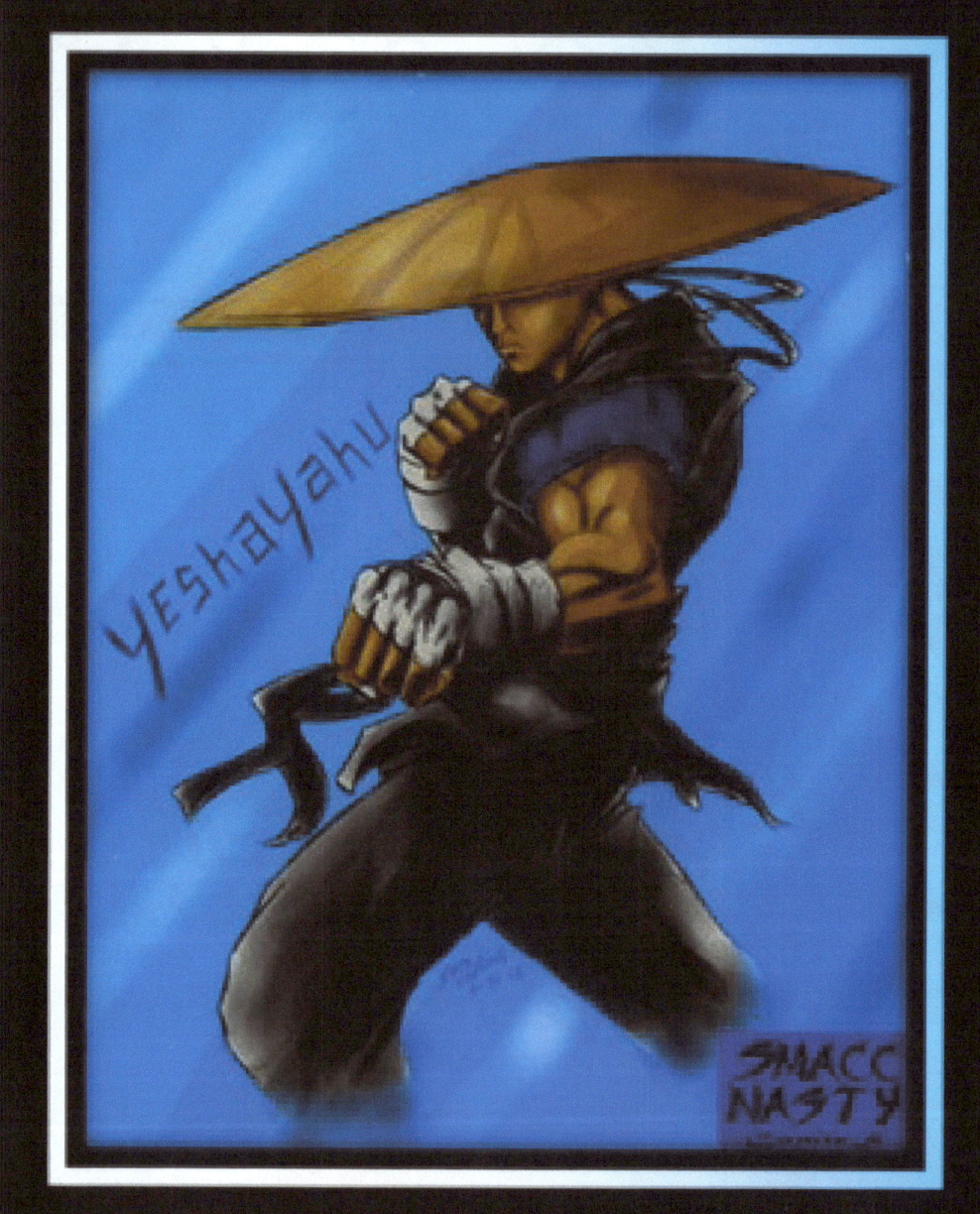

a quiet life with many female servants. All of his female servants are trained in the deadly art that he perfected called Nuba-Bujutsu. Tien Lei and his female servants are the most powerful fighters of all time. They live quietly in a heavily guarded fortress that is not on any map, but is believed to be somewhere in the continent of Asia. Tien and his "fem-fighters" train every day to defend the innocent from the demonic powers that roam the earth.

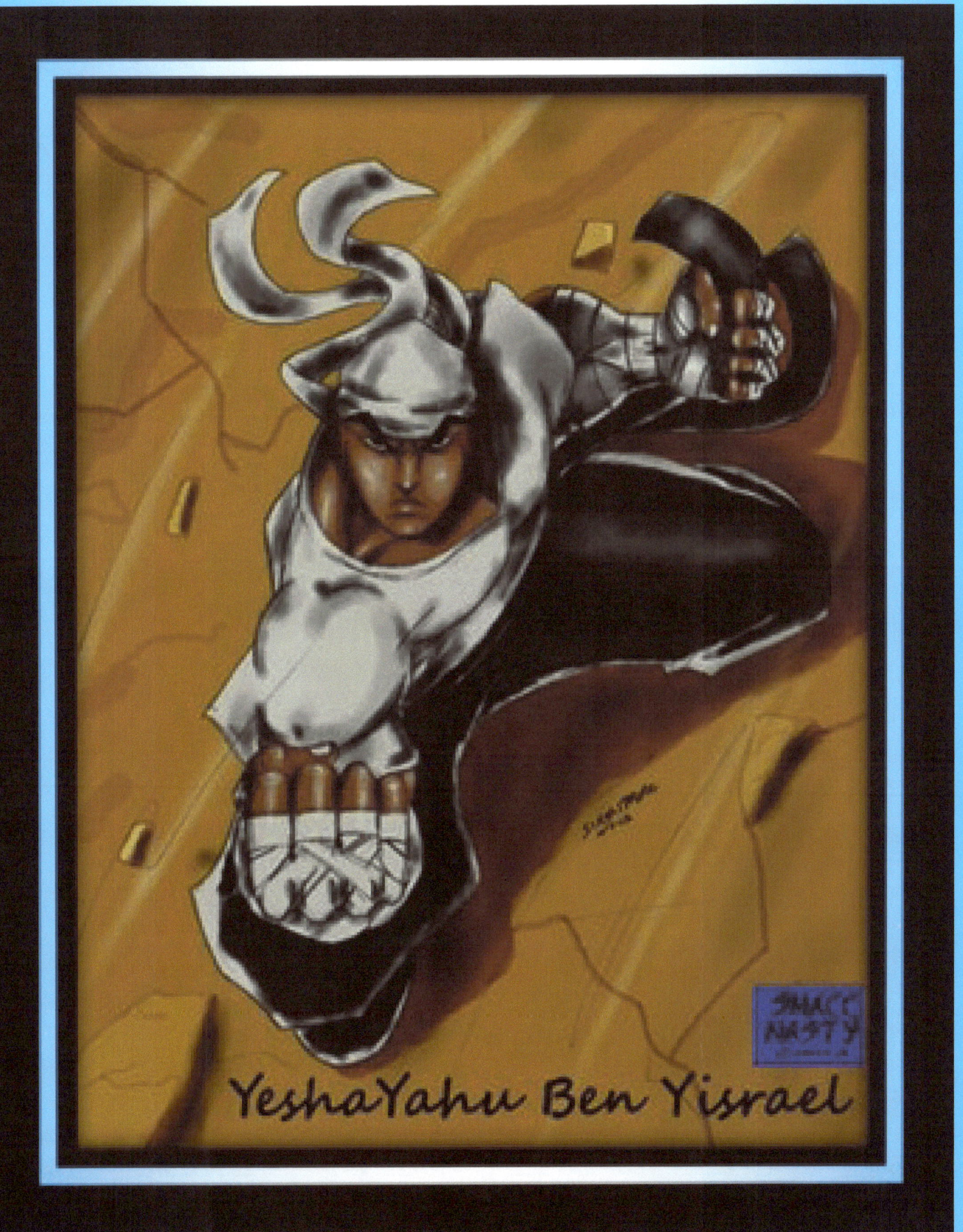

YeshaYahu Ben Yisrael

Art Gallery

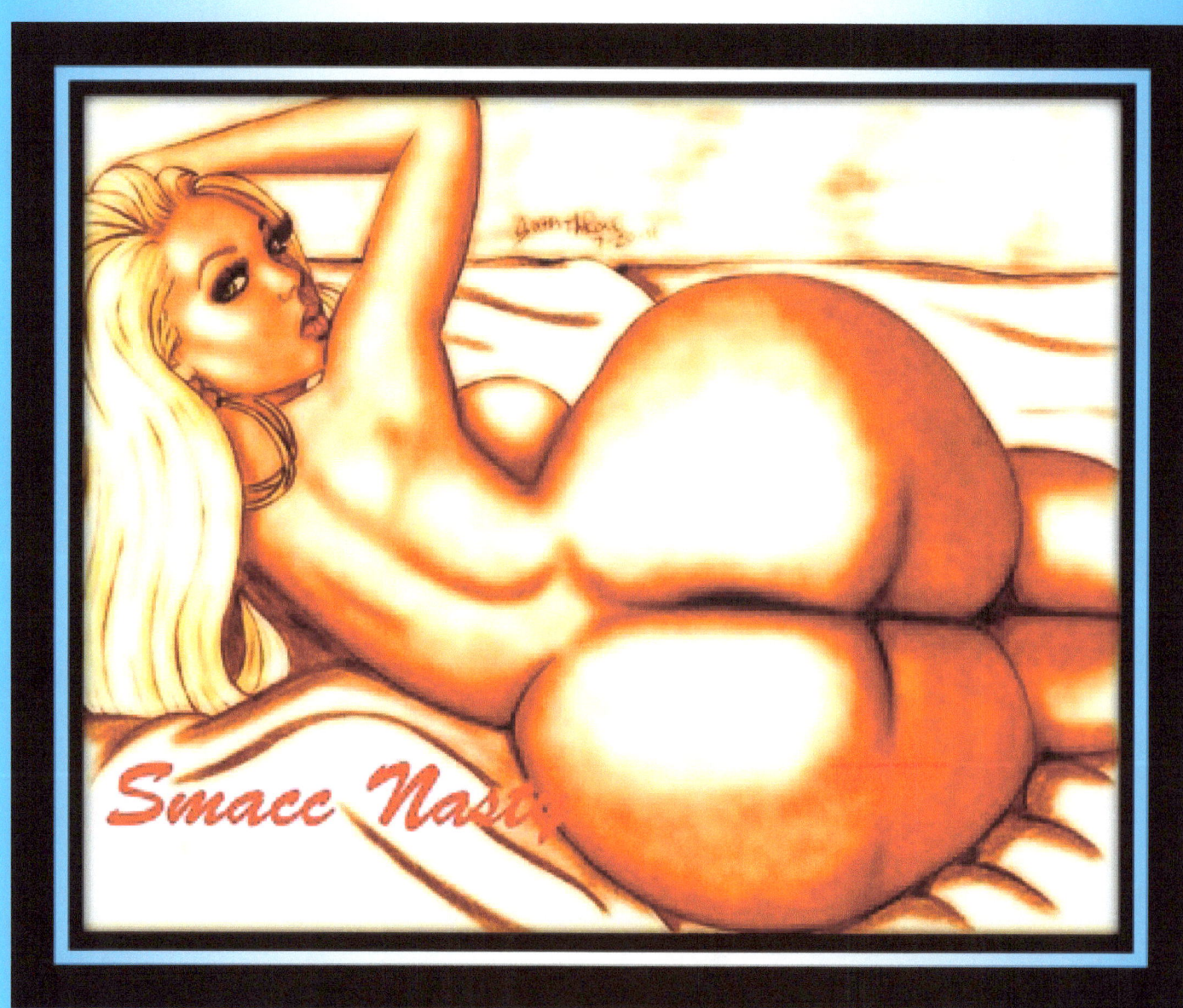

Smacc Nasty

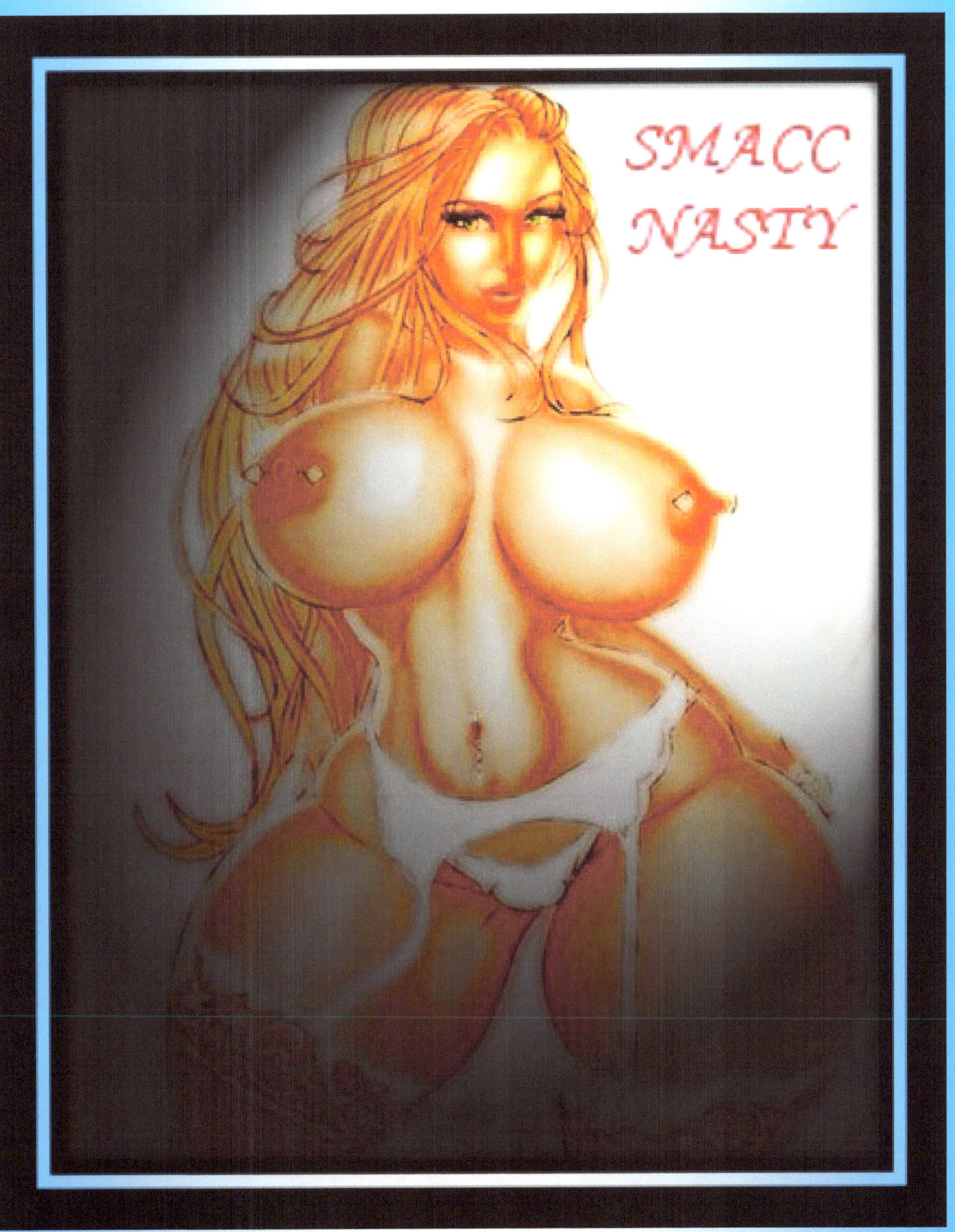

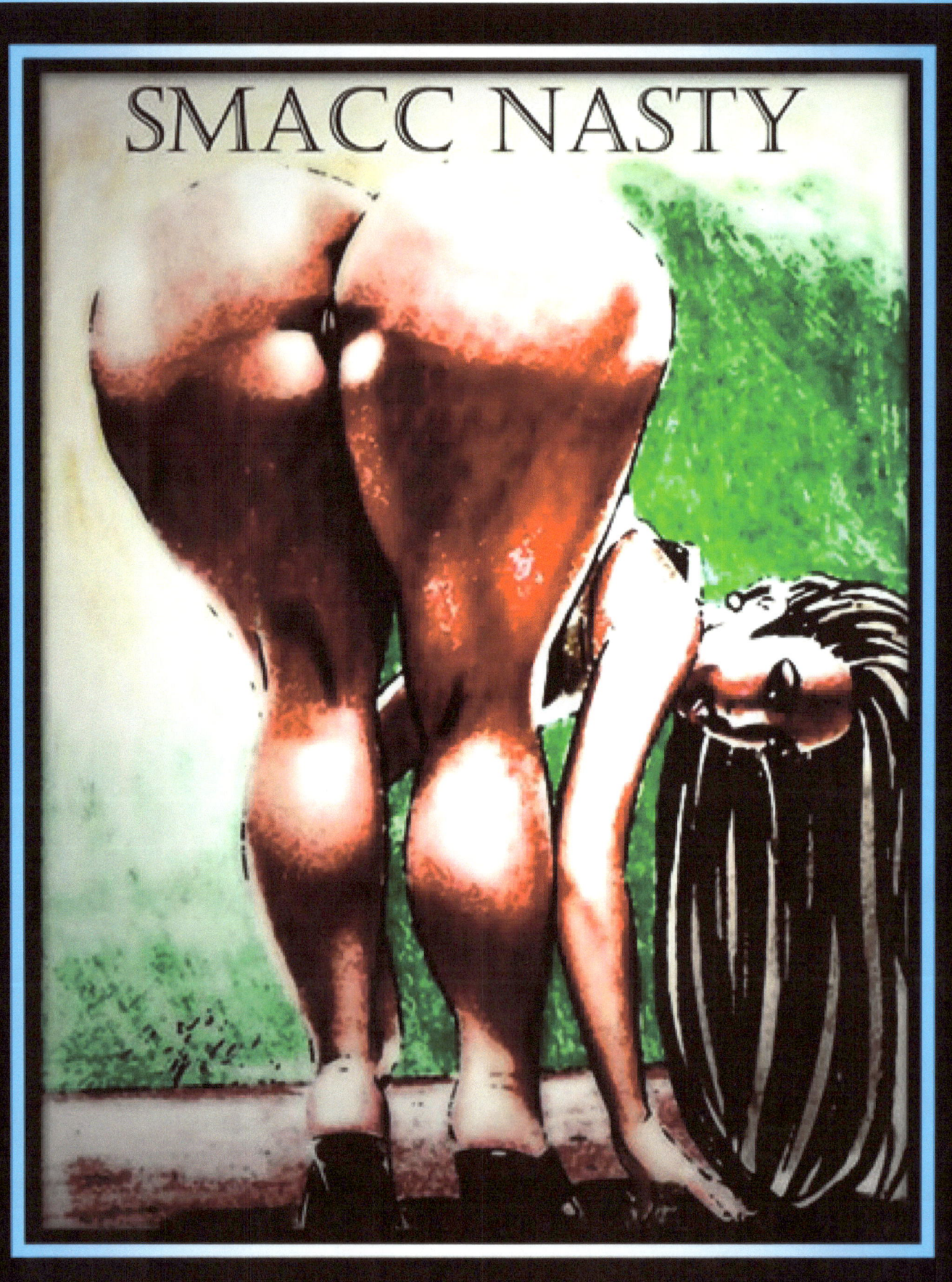

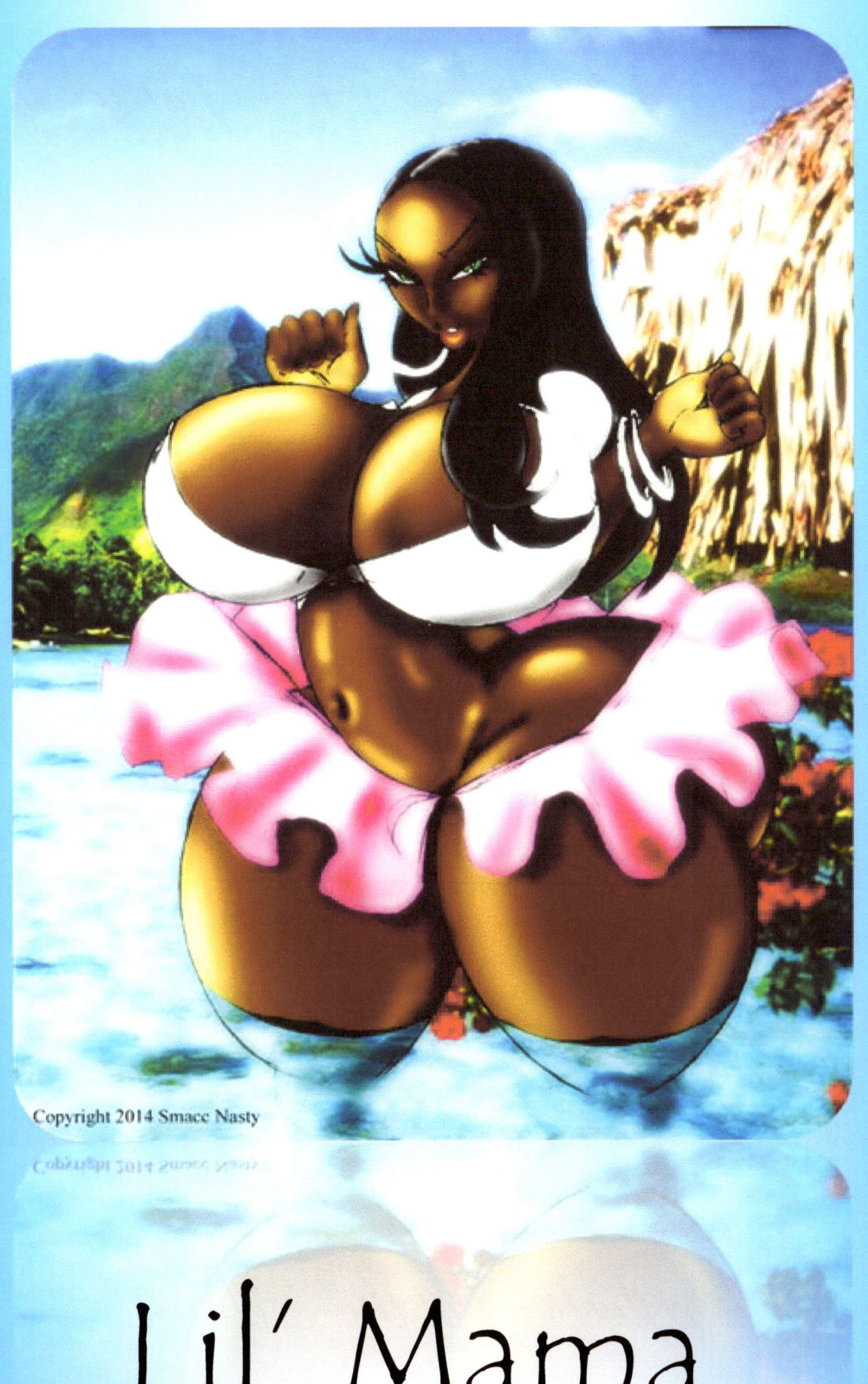

Lil' Mama

Artist: Yehezgel Ben Yisrael

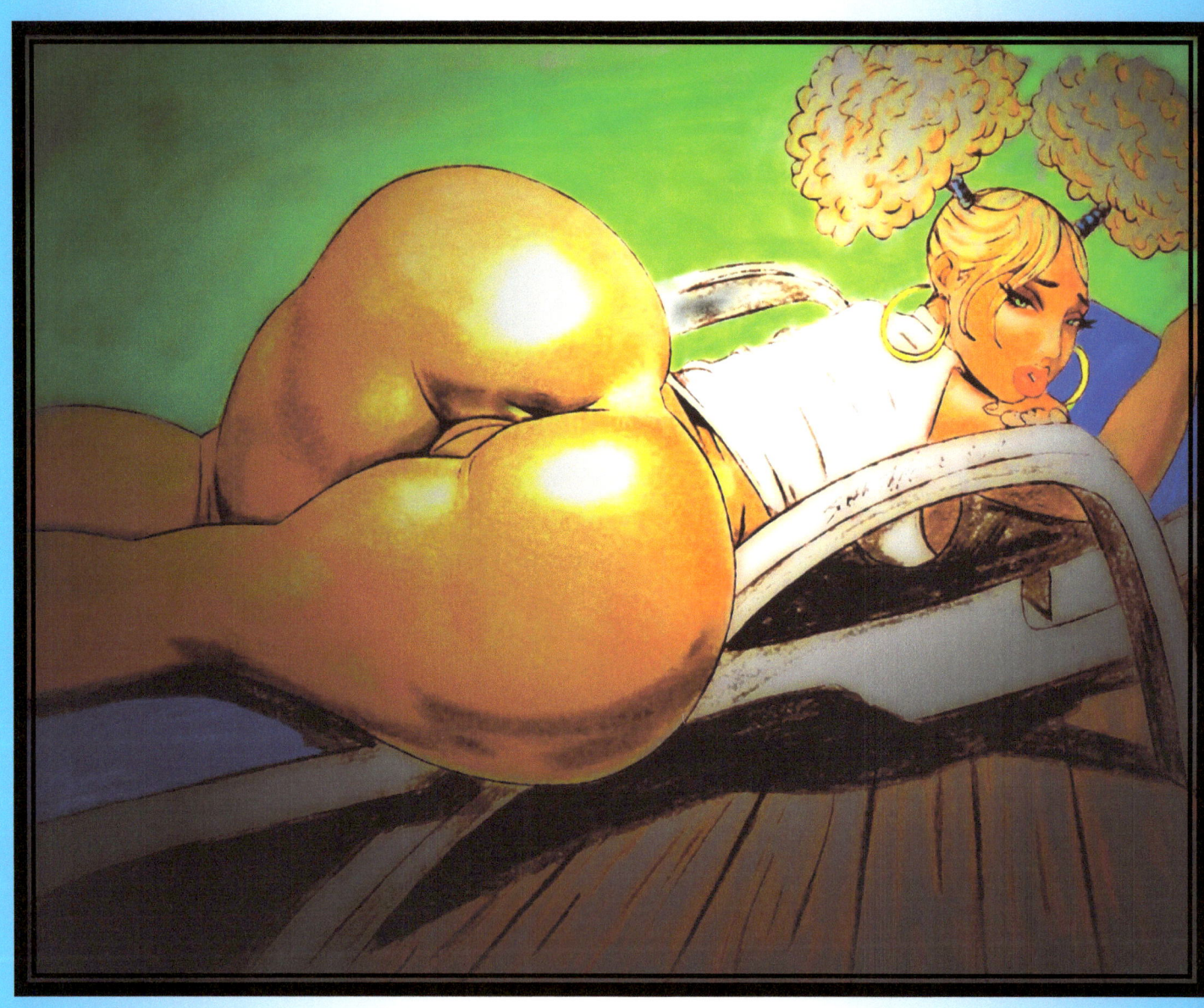

Sunlight reflects off of the Moon.

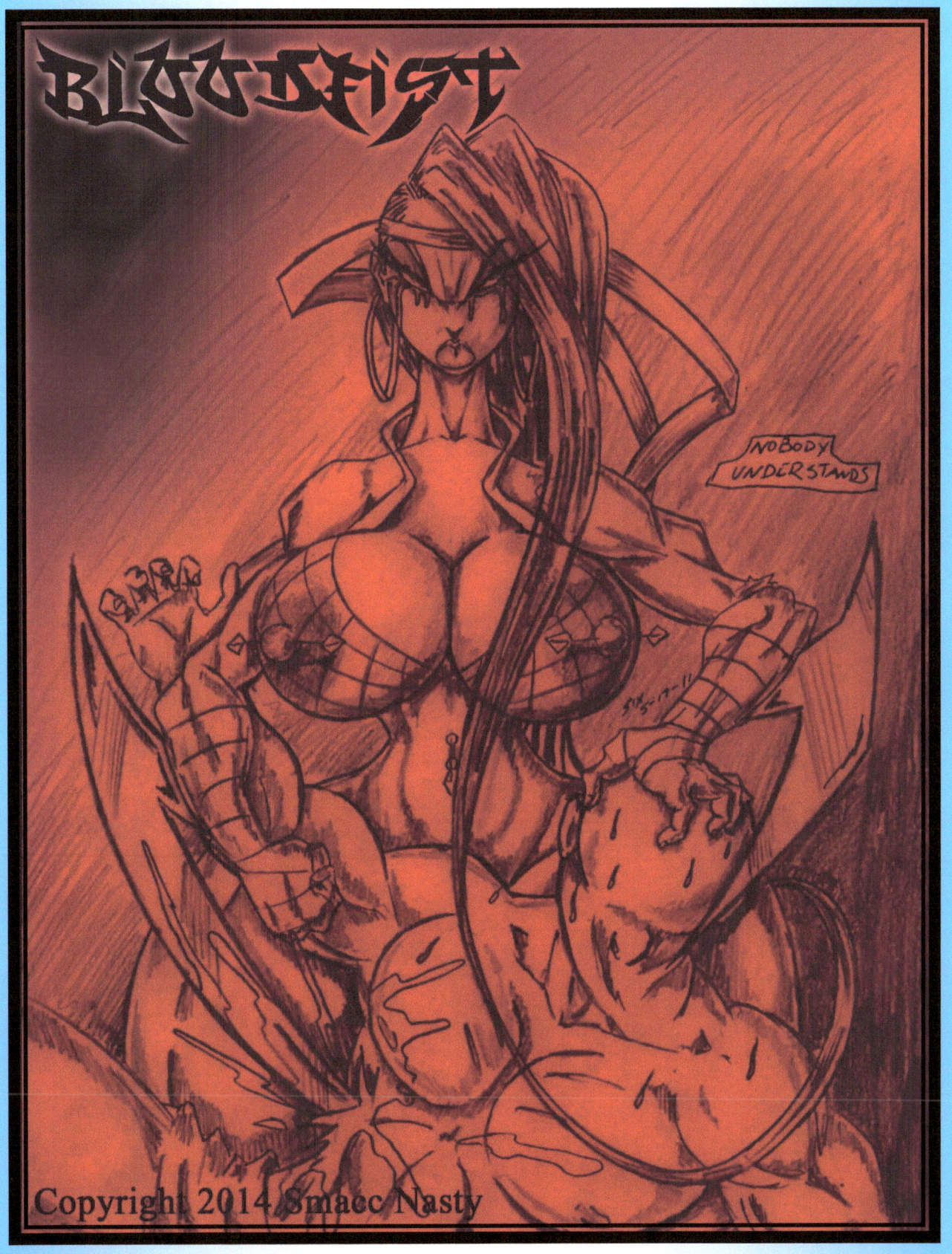

No One Understands

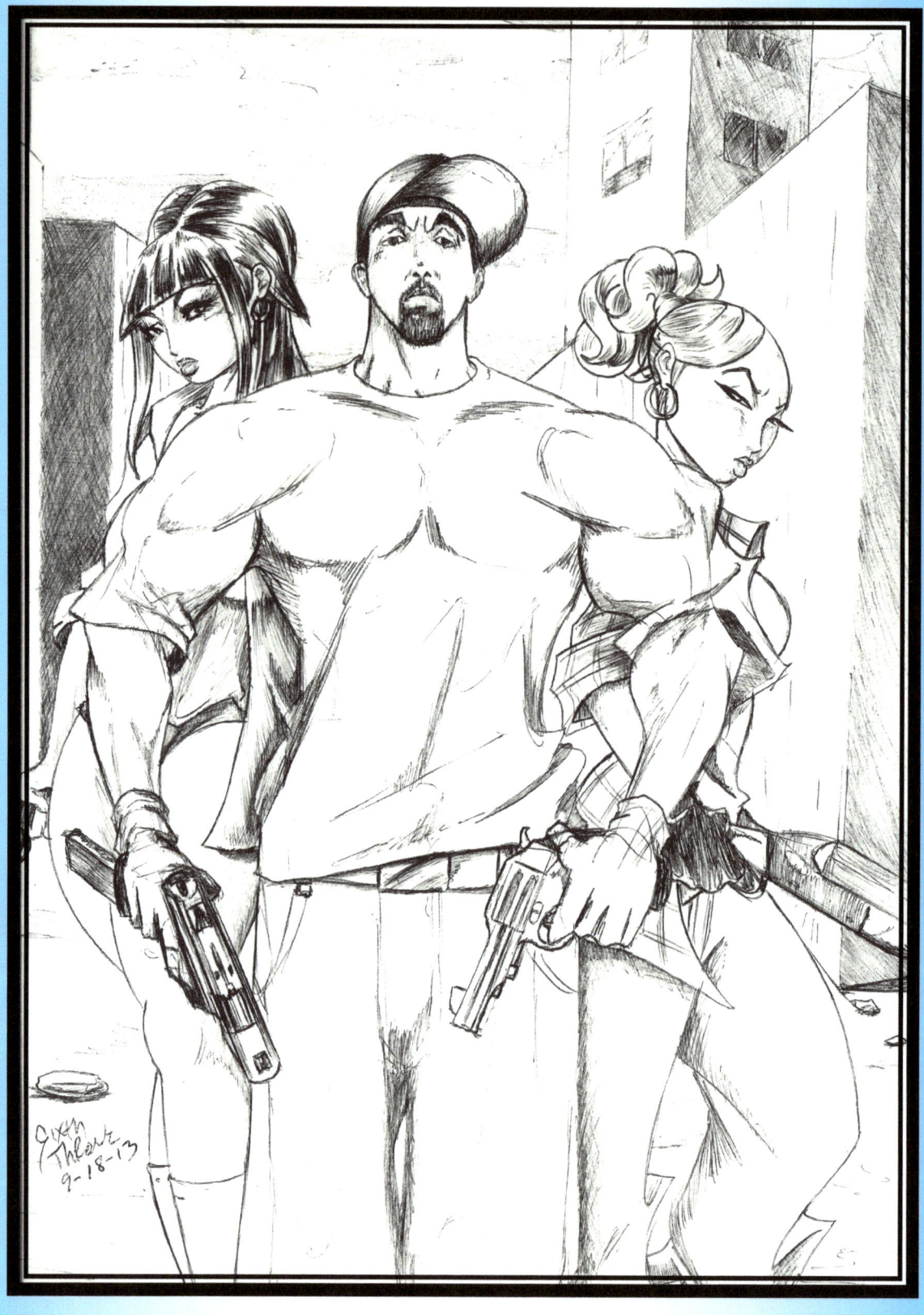

Six Throne Syndicate

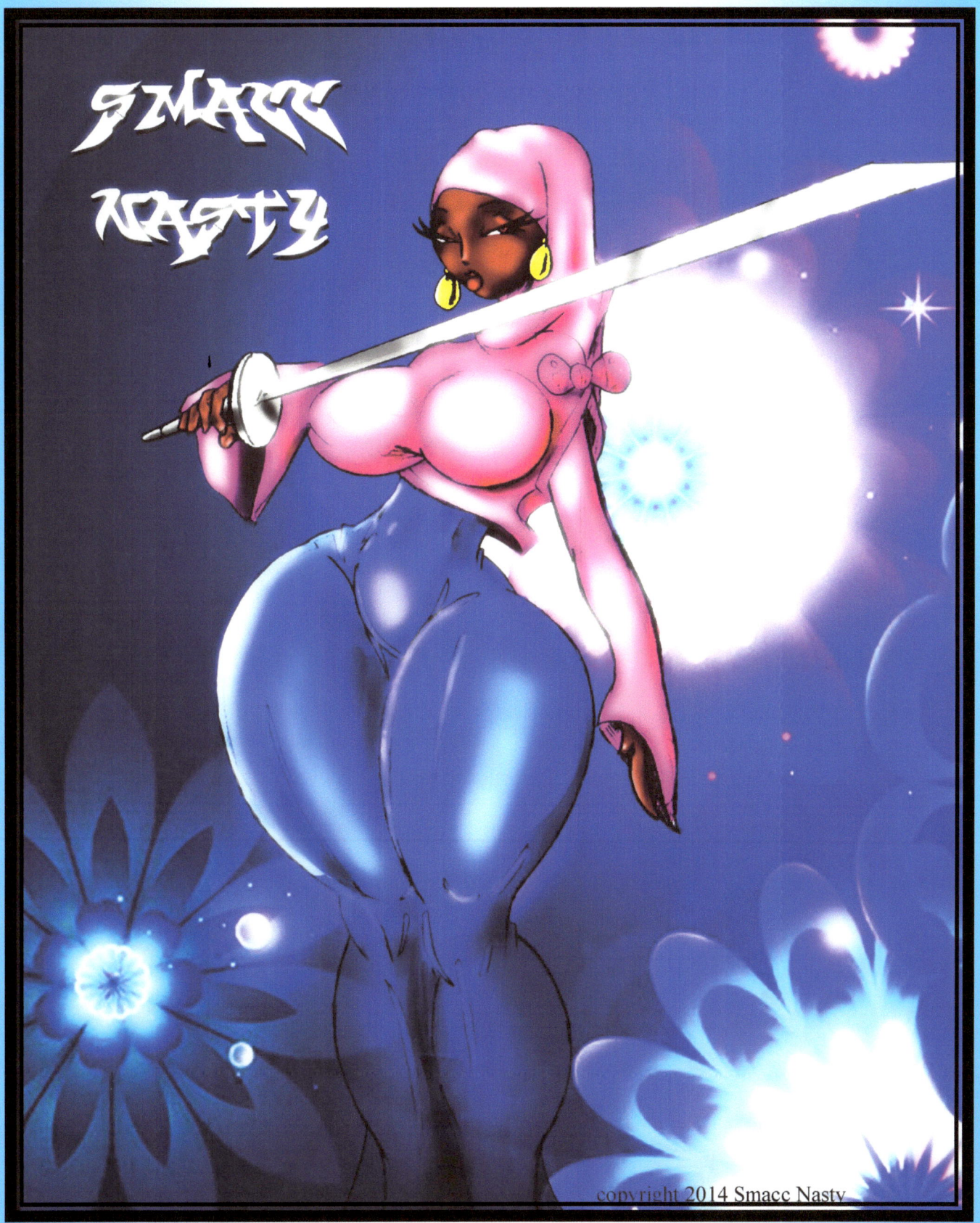

Muslimah

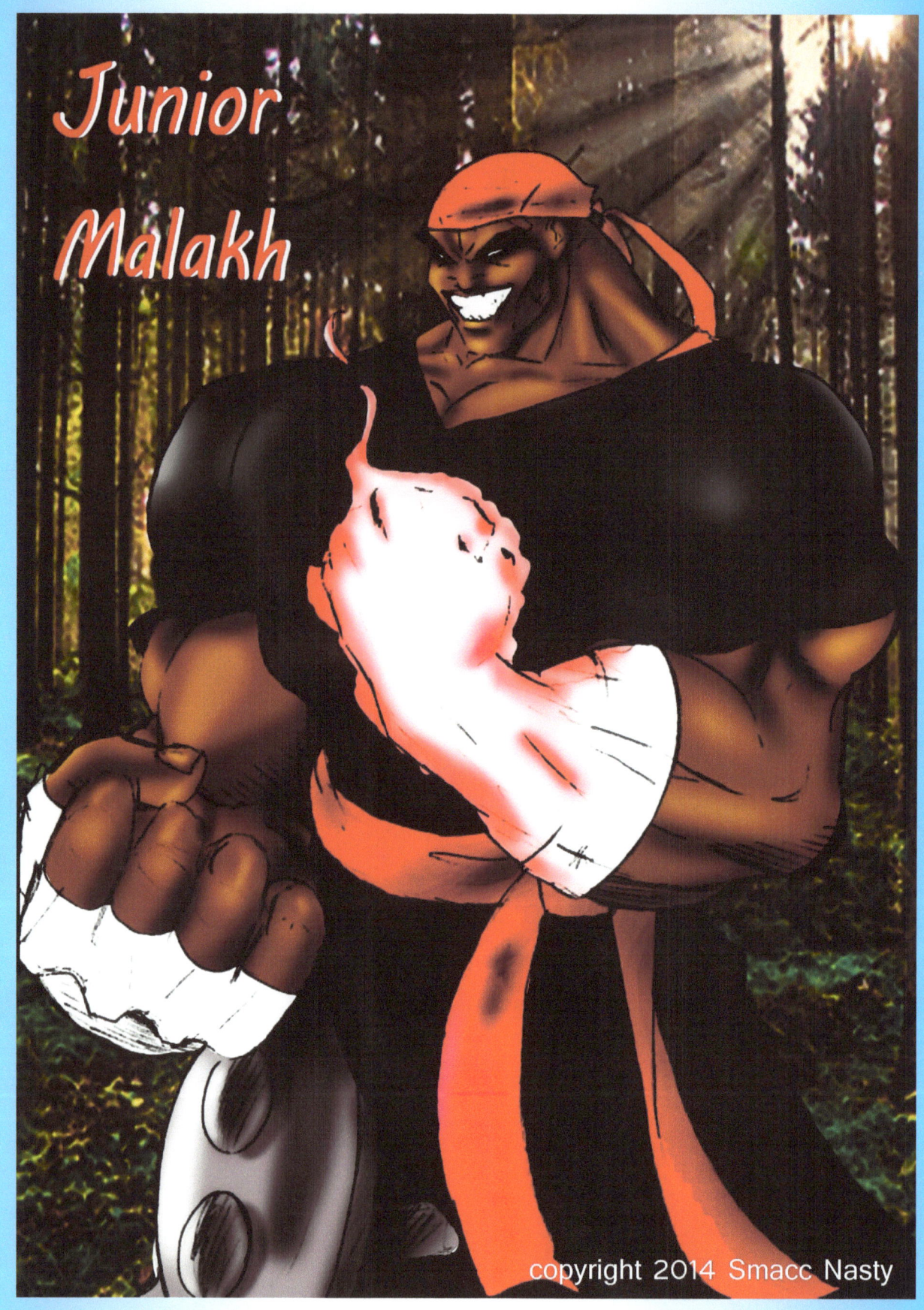

Junior Malakh

copyright 2014 Smacc Nasty

The Nephilim

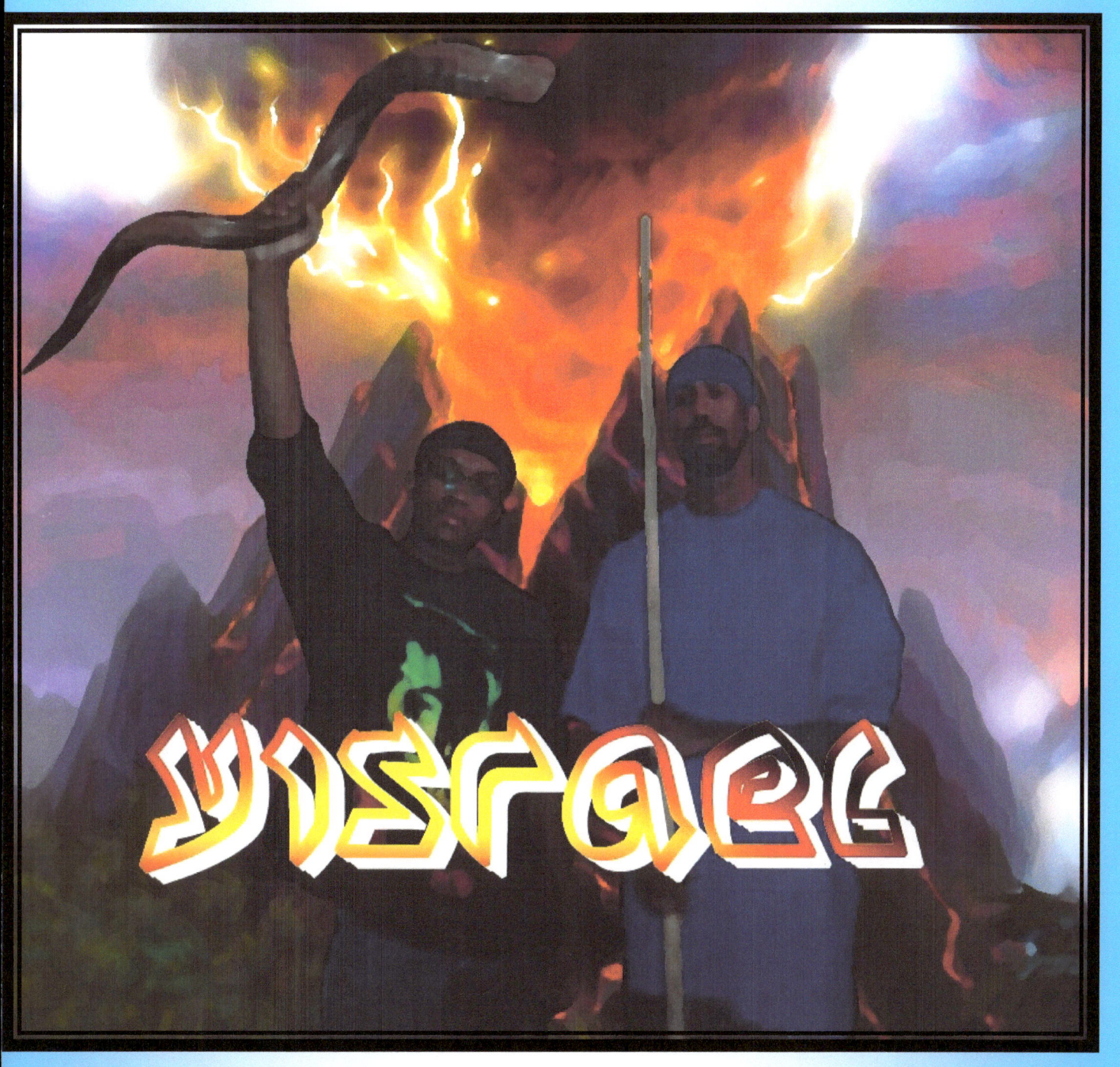

Return of Israel

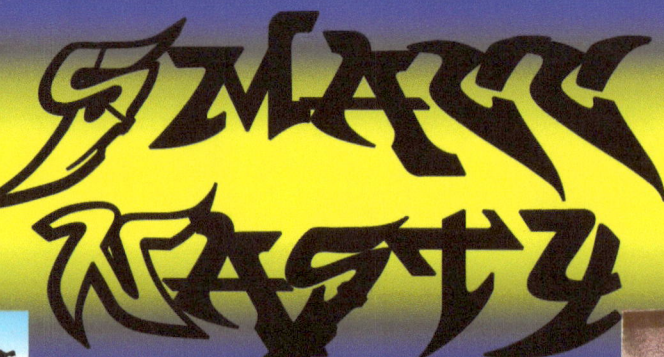

SMACC NASTY

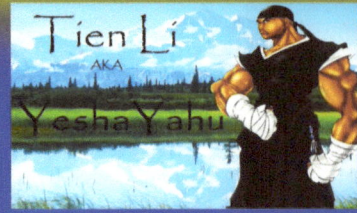

Tien Li AKA YeshaYahu

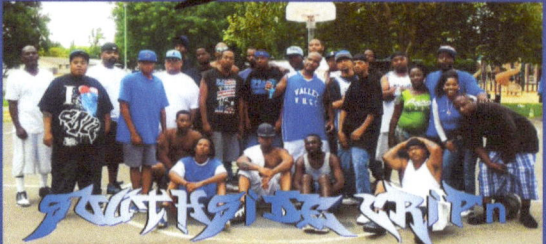

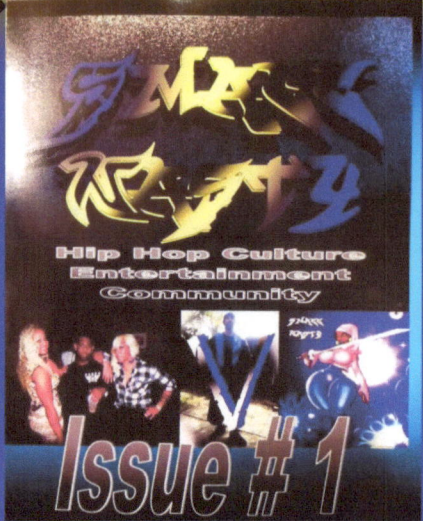

Hip Hop Culture Entertainment Community

Issue # 1

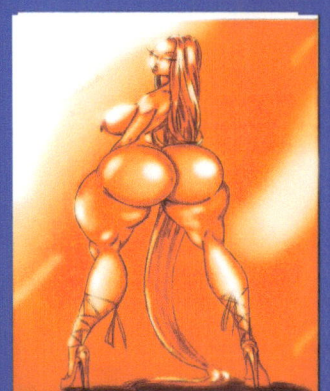

Magazine

$14.95

SMACC NASTY

DVDs

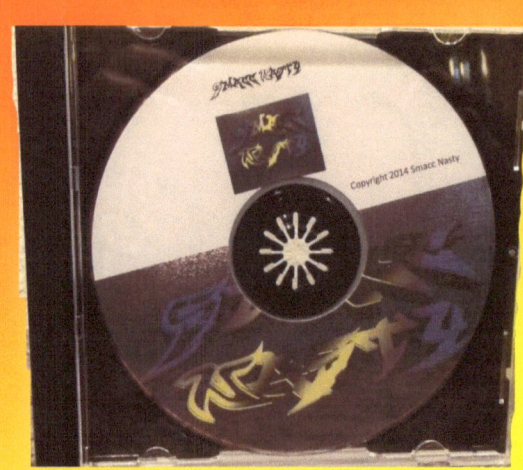

Music Videos
Performing Artist

$9.99

Smacc Nasty

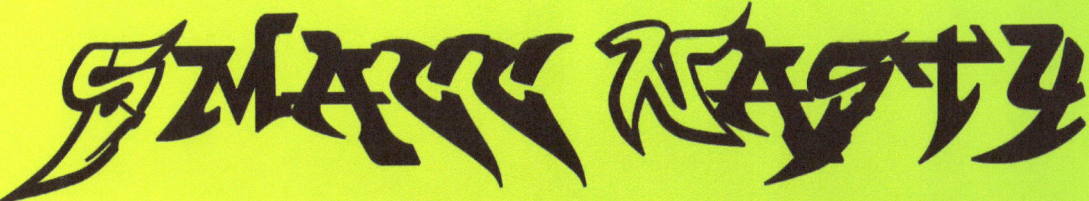

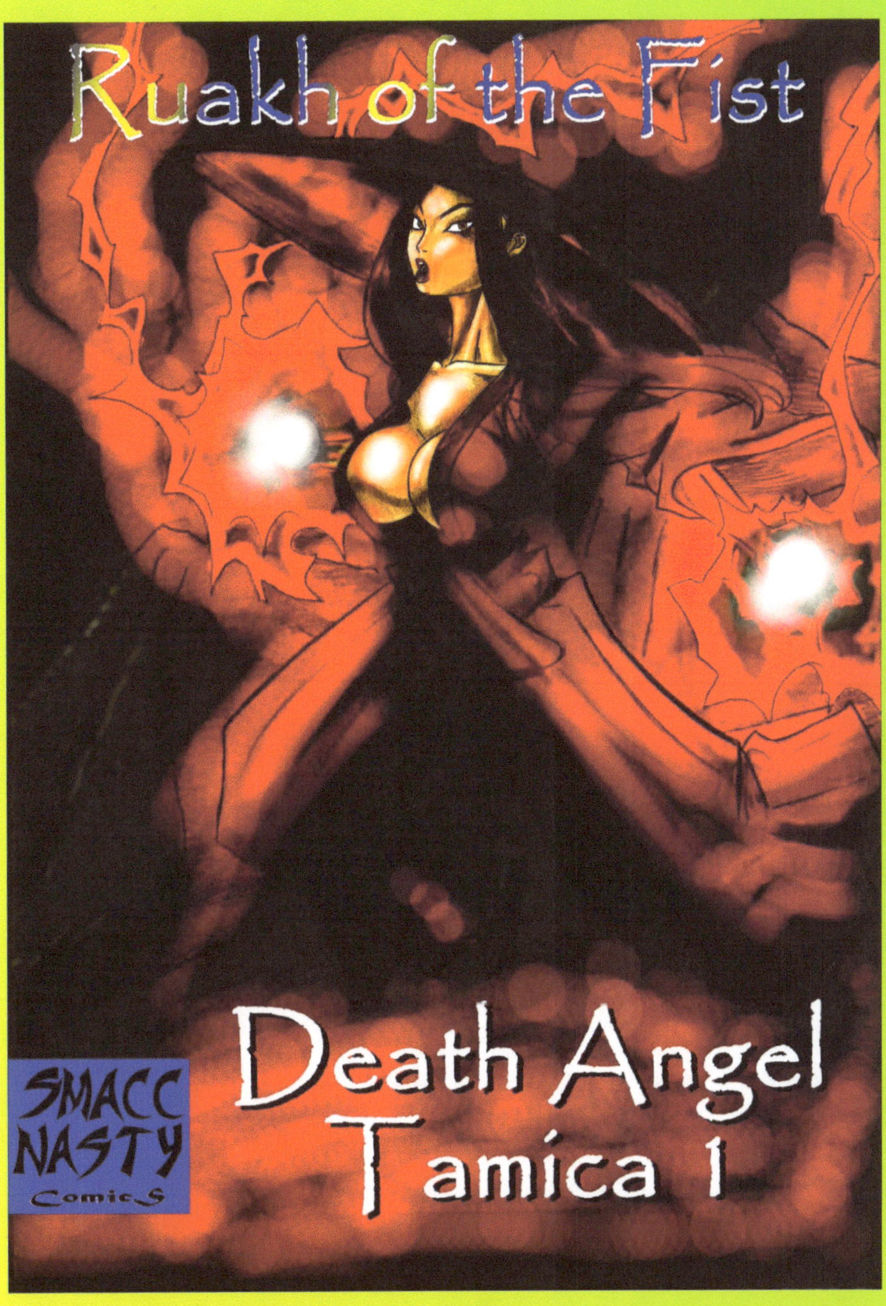